D0226168

SOCIAL RESEARCH

SOCIAL RESEARCH

THE CRAFT OF FINDING OUT

J. L. SIMMONS
GEORGE J. McCALL

University of Missouri, St. Louis

MACMILLAN PUBLISHING COMPANY
New York

COLLIER MACMILLAN PUBLISHERS
London

Copyright © 1985, Macmillan Publishing Company, a division of
Macmillan, Inc.

Printed in the United States of America

All rights reserved. No part of this book may be reproduced or
transmitted in any form or by any means, electronic or mechanical, including photocopying, recording, or any information storage and retrieval system, without permission in writing from
the Publisher.

Macmillan Publishing Company
866 Third Avenue, New York, New York 10022

Collier Macmillan Canada, Inc.

Library of Congress Cataloging in Publication Data

Simmons, J. L.
    Social research.

    Bibliography: p.
    Includes index.
    1. Sociology—Research.   I. McCall, George J.
II. Title.
HM48.S534   1985   301'.072   84-5774
ISBN 0-02-410520-1
Printing: 1   2   3   4   5   6   7   8
Year: 5   6   7   8   9   0   1   2   3

ISBN 0-02-410520-1

PREFACE

It has always been crucial for a human being to be "in the know" about his or her environment. This has been true in all past ages and will continue to be true in all times to come. Those who have, or can get, the answers simply do better than those who don't or can't. To know something, one has to go through some process of finding out. This process of finding something out is what this book is all about.

Finding out—doing research—is a universal human endeavor. Whatever one is doing and whatever field one is in, the fundamentals of inquiry are the same. Also, happily, the fundamentals are rather easy to grasp and to use.

In today's emerging information society it becomes ever more vital for each of us to be able to find things out and to make sense of the findings of others, if only to be a canny consumer of goods and services. And in every job field one is increasingly expected to be able to handle and evaluate data as a pro. Often the trainee struggles with the bewilderments of advanced techniques without ever having really understood the simple basics of research. The authors, having seen this happen too many times, have written this book to emphasize and explain the fundamentals.

Our theme is that the elaborate techniques of modern social research are only an extension and refinement of the universal human accomplishments of perception and evaluation. Investigations of any kind—whether done by a great scientist or an exploring child—embody the same few basic elements and are subject to the same influences leading to success or failure. The enormous advantage of the professional researcher lies entirely in how he or she handles these same elements, that is, in careful and creative respect for certain rules and guidelines that guard against missteps.

Our strategy, therefore, is to build on the reader's strengths, by discussing each element in the context of everyday inquiry to show how and why such rules and guidelines have developed to upgrade the success experienced in finding out. In the process the reader will also learn to detect and avoid many common mistakes made in investigations of any type. Statistical techniques are necessarily discussed in several chapters, but they are discussed nonstatistically. (A common mistake in books of this sort is an attempt also to teach something of statistics—quite out of context and in far too short a frame.) Research, and books about it, need not be tedious or dull. Finding out can be a fascinating human adventure, and it is presented that way within the pages of this book.

We have done our best to make this book (1) readable, (2) understandable, and (3) widely useful. We have worked and done research mostly in the social sciences over the past twenty-five years, so most of our emphasis and examples come from these fields. Yet, we have tried to distill and communicate the basics of the research process, to help anyone in any sort of finding-out venture.

A book is always to some degree the product of an interpersonal network, so we owe some acknowledgements to some people in ours. We thank our wives Nola and Nancy for their forbearance while we worked on the manuscript. Nola Simmons did an outside reading of the draft and provided many useful suggestions. Our colleagues, students, and research coworkers over the years have provided a continuing roundtable on the promises, pleasures, and pitfalls of finding out. And finally we thank our editor, James D. Anker, who has provided one of the cleanest, most straightforward, and positive editorial experiences we have ever encountered in the publishing business.

Our book is dedicated to the propositions that real knowledge is the best antidote for the ills of humanity and that our wheel of collective human intelligence could roll forward into a better world.

J. L. Simmons

George J. McCall

CONTENTS

P A R T
III
MODES OF SOCIAL RESEARCH

PART
IV
CREATIVE INQUIRY

15
THE CRAFT OF FINDING OUT 145

LIST OF FIGURES

PART
I

ESSENTIALS

All of us continually engage in the process of reaching out into our environments to find out. In this basic sense we are all researchers. The process of finding things out is fundamentally similar for the layman and the scientist. The professional researcher refines and extends our universal human activities of perceiving and evaluating slices of the world by developing guidelines and procedures that maximize the yield of knowledge gained while minimizing the errors made. Researchers embrace these rules and routines because they have proved more workable than any others yet developed by humanity for getting at the truth. There is no monopoly on these guidelines; anyone can use them, in any sphere of inquiry, from the street to the stars.

Knowledge won from research ventures into the environment is sometimes kept personal, but is often shared with others so that our collective understandings continue to accumulate in every field. This is the wheel of collective human intelligence that has delivered to us all the wonders of modern science and technology.

In the process of living, we are all at least amateur researchers. This book is dedicated to the improvement of these skills.

CHAPTER

1

TRUTHS AND CONSEQUENCES

The environment we inhabit is sometimes exciting, sometimes demanding, but always there and quite real. It continuously impinges on us and in turn we continuously shape and influence it, knowingly or thoughtlessly. So we must know about it. If we don't know, we must find out.

Probably few people would sit down in the evening and, just for fun, read a book on how to do research. Yet everyone, from the smallest child to the professional scientist, is engaged in research—in finding out things about their environment, at least in their own daily lives. Success in such investigations can bring a multitude of rewards, while failures can be costly, even fatal. Shoppers, businessmen, and scientists all need to come up with right answers, so it is worthwhile for anyone to increase their understanding of how good research is done. Most people balk at learning about research because "that's something that specialists do" and because research techniques may look complicated and forbidding. But, however complex the techniques may appear to be, the basic essentials of research technology can be easily understood and used. So be of good cheer.

If a person has some grasp of the basic principles underlying research investigation, he or she can

- win more and lose less in their own career and personal life.
- make much better use of the floods of research results pouring out in all fields in today's information society.

• more easily go on to learn the specific research technologies that are becoming a vital aspect of all professions.

Let us start out with an interesting point about learning the technology of research. You already are a fairly decent investigator and evaluator, or you never would have survived in the environment long enough to be here studying this book. If you had not correctly appraised your environment thousands of times, if you had not drawn a vast number of more or less correct conclusions from your perceptions of the world, you wouldn't have made it this far in life. So, congratulations.

You've also, no doubt, had many failures along the way. It may come as a surprise that the majority of these failures have been the result of some fundamental research error. Learning about such research errors and how to minimize them can cut your future losses.

Research techniques are actually an outgrowth and refinement of what human beings ordinarily do in their continual quest to understand things. Research is done to find out about the environment, and social research is done to find out about the social environment. Research methods are not some alien science; they are distilled from the universal human experience of navigating the environment, whether the snowy rim of nothern Alaska or the streets of Philadelphia. Thus, all living persons are daily engaged in at least rudimentary forms of research into the world around them. Which store has the best food for the money? What stocks will be good long-term investments? What's the story on the new girl? What to do about a leaky bathroom faucet? What's wrong with the car now? Such kinds of questions are continually posed, and some sort of answers are worked out. Those who have the edge in getting good answers are usually more successful in the business of living than their fellows. But anyone can improve his or her investigative skills.

The truth is, most people do a rather poor job of finding answers to their questions, compared with what they could do if only they had more understanding of research essentials. Far too often they accept opinion as fact and hearsay as hard evidence; they are swayed by advertising hype as much as by actual product performance; they uncritically accept the packaged answers floating about in their culture and within their social circles. When they set out on their own to find something out, their questions are often vague, their samplings of the environment are slanted, their data gathering is haphazard, their analysis is hit-and-miss, and their evaluations are made on the basis of whim as much as reasoning. A glance at virtually anyone's career and personal life demonstrates that he or she would benefit from improved investigative skills. Increased understanding of the essentials of research will not necessarily make one into an Einstein or a Sherlock Holmes; neither will it guarantee that one will make a fortune in the stock market or pick the best dentist. But it certainly will help.

Learning to make evaluations involves understanding research essentials. We are all continuously bombarded with information, expert opinions, explanations, recommendations, and advice from a host of near and distant terminals in today's emerging Information Society. A person must evaluate this flood of often conflicting facts and claims in order to navigate the contemporary scene. Statistics can not only lie but they can cheat and steal. Meanwhile, promotional and propaganda techniques have been raised to a fine art in our time. So this book is also intended to make readers more canny consumers of others' researches. How many times have we acted innocently on the findings of others to our later sorrow?

THE PROFESSIONAL DIFFERENCE

Research methods are actually an extension, refinement, and codification of the ordinary processes involved in human intelligence—the accurate perceiving and evaluating of the environment that even the most primitive tribes and small children continually carry out. The very notion of intellect refers to the ability to perceive, reason, and understand; intelligence refers to the ability to learn or understand from experience.

Any intelligent being, whether child or research scientist, is inquisitive, and the process of inquiry has many fundamental similarities. Each individual

- has some sort of interest or question, founded in some way on prior knowledge or beliefs.
- has some resources and resource limits.
- has some sort of approach to finding out information that will satisfy that interest or question.
- samples the environment in some fashion to gather data.

- examines the obtained data and draws from them some conclusions and implications.

Any operating human being embodies the seeds of modern research technology.

So why aren't we all natural research scientists? Despite the similarities noted, there must be some crucial differences between the ordinary layman and the scientific investigator. The answer is that the research scientist has learned the rules and techniques worked out by generations of inquirers, to the point where he or she has become a *professional* inquirer. This is the crucial difference between scientific research and ordinary inquiry. This is all that bars "primitives," children, and ordinary laymen from doing social research, or nuclear research.

Most of us doctor ourselves to a considerable extent, but when things get risky or serious, the fear of error leads us to turn to a professional physician. Most of us can do some fixing up around the house, but beyond a certain point we call in a professional repairman. Similarly, we are all fairly skilled at everyday inquiry, by ordinary standards, but amateurs—sloppy, error-prone, and unreliable—by professional standards of research.

The professional researcher's quest to find something out is conducted according to a pretty much agreed upon set of guidelines and principles—rules of the game. Mind you, these are not rules in the sense of endlessly detailed regulations manuals that one must quote and memorize. Nor are they red tape to hassle the investigator. The rules of research are no more sacred than the rules of backgammon or carpentry; they just happen to have worked out better, more often, and more predictably during the course of human history than other sorts of rules for inquiry. For example, it pays to verify one's hunches by checking them out with hard data before investing one's life savings or launching a new medical treatment. Application of these rules has delivered all the miracles of modern science into our hands, so they have proved their merit. They do not replace human creativity, but are actually designed to harness and augment it. And best of all, perhaps, these guidelines and principles can be learned and used by virtually anyone.

A human being, by nature, seems to be a marvelously but imperfectly intelligent creature. Experts in artificial intelligence (the designers of computers and robots) marvel at the flexibility, responsiveness, and self-awareness of the human mind. Yet experts on human intelligence find many problems and failings:

- Human beliefs are resistant to contrary evidence.
- Human perception, attention, and memory are sharply limited and systematically biased.
- Humans have a high tolerance for ambiguity, inconsistency, and error.
- Humans tend to be rather poor at formal reasoning, compared with even a pocket calculator.
- Humans do not adequately share useful information or accept it from others.

Make no mistake about it; the professional researcher is as prone to all these failings as the person in the street. What mainly sets apart the professional is his or her skill in applying the guidelines and principles this book will examine. What the ordinary inquirer does intuitively and perhaps unconsciously, the professional does consciously, objectively, recordably, and according to plan.

ORGANIZED APPROACH TO INQUIRY

The professional investigator employs an organized approach to inquiry, utilizing established guidelines that have proved so successful. For example, there are rules of evidence; hunches and rumors might be worth following up, but these must be verified by hard evidence. There are coherent techniques for data gathering and analysis that cannot be set aside on a whim. Empiricism (what really is) takes precedence over belief or wish, whether you like the findings or not. Whatever conclusions may be reached are then put through rigorous evaluation and verification procedures by the rest of the research community. One can often find at least rudimentary forms of all such rules in the activities of those people who are especially successful in some field. An astute policeman or a good journalist or a canny investor will, for example, display traces of them in their work. The professional researcher simply is trained to use them knowingly, explicitly, and consistently.

Chapter 2 will look into the nature of research, how it relates to the wheel of collective human intelligence, and the research errors and biases that bedevil the layman and professional alike. Part II will take up each of the eight basic elements of research in turn to see how they weave together throughout the research process. Part III will examine each of the four major modes of social research developed collectively by the scientific community over the centuries to find out the truth. Part IV will examine the craft of researching.

One other point—the professional researcher is not a windup mechanical robot. The mechanical aspects of research—the countings and codings and cross-analyses—are often overemphasized in textbooks on the subject. The research process is presented as a neat, logical sequence of steps, leading from posed hypothesis to drawn conclusions.

Almost no research project follows such a neat, rationalistic pattern. The realities of finding out, like all human endeavors, often stray pretty far from the textbook versions. However, the rules of the game remain as the guidelines throughout a real-world investigation. So this book will look at many of the factors surrounding research, as well as the idealized process, because research never occurs in a social vacuum.

Research is not a dull, plodding affair; it is a venture, often an adventure. Like any venture, it entails some routine chores, but these do not deserve the whole of one's attention. This book will address the venture, as well as the chores.

CHAPTER

2

THE NATURE OF RESEARCH

The professional researcher can perhaps best be described as a cross between a scholar and an adventurer. Interestingly, many researchers display this hybrid mix in their personal lives. Their lives often tend to be colorful because they poke around and venture into areas beyond the well-established domains of knowledge and understanding. Like Marco Polos, they return from their journeys to tell the rest of the world what they have found. Views of reality are often expanded and changed as a result.

In social research, as in ordinary inquiry, the aim is to bring about a closer correspondence between empirical realities (what really is) and our conceptual models of them (what we think things are). All human beings operate on the basis of some internal model of the world around them, relying on this model in their thinking, planning, and actions. Such models may be conscious or unconscious, well organized or disjointed, and based upon superstition, forceful indoctrination, or the best scientific reasoning. But everyone has such internal models. How well these conceptions fit and explain realities is the measure of how smart and successful the individual or group will be.

We want to find out the truth, or at least a truth, about something. But we cannot proceed directly between concepts and realities. Inquiry is the bridge between the two.

There is a looping interdependence among ideas, the empirical world, and researches. These three do not form any kind of a straight-line sequence; rather, they are more like three points on a wheel, where one can move across from any one point to any other. Also, one may enter this circle at any of the three points (Figure 1). The continuing interplays among theory, reality, and research hold true for amateur and professional inquirers alike. For instance, the great increase in sexual assault rates (reality) has cast grave doubts upon the theory advanced by some that liberalization of sexual attitudes would markedly reduce such crimes. Facts may force us to do research resulting in new theories. Or our theories may give birth to a particular research line that uncovers hitherto unsuspected facts. And so on, in all possible combinations. Each point on the circle is capable of bringing about changes in the other two. For example, new concepts may lead to new technologies, which in turn change realities, as have the telephone and the automobile.

The rules and routines of research are designed to keep this wheel of collective human intelligence running straight and upward toward ever-increasing understandings of our universe. The fact that these increased understandings may then produce changes in the environment only means that we then will have new realities to inquire about.

The quest for understanding must be an active pursuit, because an environment will seldom, if ever, automatically give up its truths. Truth, of course, can sometimes be cruel. It is often the enemy of illusions and sometimes the enemy of one's hopes and dreams. Some people don't really want to know, at least about some things, because their conceptual models might then be in jeopardy. On the other side, many people don't want others to know certain things, for one reason or another. So, particularly in the social sciences the environ-

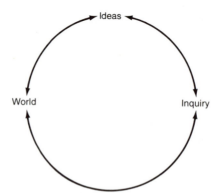

FIGURE 1. Relations Among Concepts, Empirical Reality, and Research

ment may not be very cooperative in giving up its truths. Cooperation from the environment must usually be negotiated in some fashion, even in the physical sciences. And, because we don't yet know the answers, our preliminary ideas about the areas under investigation are always more limited than the realities they address. Our notions of some foreign society, or even of the people living "on the other side of the tracks," are, for example, almost inevitably simplistic and stereotyped.

Hence, on our research trail of truth, we almost inevitably encounter scenes behind scenes, sometimes more fabulous than any fantasy fiction. For example, a personal relationship or a nation's diplomatic moves are seldom what they appear to be on the surface. This "veils of reality" phenomenon is often the case, in subjects ranging from astronomy to international politics to the world behind the front door of our neighbor's house. The researcher is perennially striving to be "in the know" about the real scene, whether it be the rings of Saturn, the story behind a crisis headline, or how illegal aliens really operate.

In the social realm, the actual live scenes usually lie behind some screening of public relations and social front. The most familiar example of this is probably the continual discrepancies between what people say and what they are actually thinking while they say it. Inquiry into the real scene is probably as old as gossip and no doubt forms the basis for the popularity of media exposés and intimate biographies. People are looking for the "real story."

Without the real story, our theories about any slice of the environment will be askew, and any plans based upon them will be at risk. How does an organization really operate? What factors really contribute to a successful relationship? What situation is actually causing all the patient's symptoms? How are major political candidates actually chosen? How do successful single parents really manage? What is the real extent and hazard level of our toxic wastes problem? What is the basis of the strange experiences of patients pronounced clinically dead who return to life? The research trail to the actual workings of some areas is often twisty, even masked by misdirections on the part of its inhabitants. Our research rules are the guidebooks that carry us through.

The degree of correspondence between some reality and our conceptions of it is the degree of truth we have reached. But this still leaves us mostly at the level of description. We also usually want to explain and predict. To do this, we must find out some of the *regularities* in an area and the relationships among these regular features. Even at the workaday level we want to know, for instance, will shopping at Sunbath Supermarket routinely give us decent food at lower prices, or will mild daily exercise and nutritional supplements significantly contribute to our health? Hence, description is always necessary but seldom sufficient to tell us what we want to know. So we formulate notions (hypotheses) that can be explicitly checked out and verified, modifed, or thrown away.

One mark of a professional investigator, in science or in life, is that he or she needs less data to draw useful conclusions. You can see this with good professional workmen: a skilled, experienced plumber or dentist does a quick inspection, gets a few bits of data, locates the problem, draws some conclusions, and proceeds with handling the problem, all in one fluid sequence. In such cases there is a high degree of correspondence between the workman's conceptual models and the real situations he or she is investigating and handling. Interestingly, this can serve as a rough yardstick of the state of some particular science or technology—the degree to which an ordinary, trained practitioner can effectively investigate and handle a situation within his or her area of specialization.

As we look at an investigation of any sort, we can begin to see the many interplays among theory, research, and reality. In any inquiry, we almost never have to start from scratch, knowing nothing, having no concepts about the realities we are investigating. There are always some pre-existing notions floating around. In modern times, with rapidly accumulating information, we at least have some rudimentary background notions, and usually some general knowledge from others' previous investigations. Such prior knowledge may, of course, turn out to be wrong, but at least it provides some kind of starting point. Think how vast this accumulated collective information is, compared with what, for instance, an unsocialized person raised in isolation would have. Seldom, if ever, does the modern researcher go into any area without some model built from previous work. Hence we are usually concerned with an extension, elaboration, refinement, or testing of what we already think we know. Such refinements, however, can take very startling turns, such as the discovery that the earth is round, the development of the electronic chip, the finding of black holes, or the emergence of a nationwide senior citizens' subculture.

In the social and policy sciences, our conceptual models are still a fuzzy and incomplete sampling of the territories. We have learned a great deal in the last few decades, but researchers and practitioners alike have far more questions than answers.

ELEMENTARY PERCEPTIONS

The most elementary level of research (and of ordinary inquiry) is simply where one accurately perceives some segment of the environment and draws some correct conclusions from these perceptions. For instance, one looks out the window and gathers a multitude of perceptions (data) that are swiftly and subliminally coded and analyzed to yield the summary facts that it's raining hard, the ground is muddy, and the sky is lighter over in the direction the rain is coming from. One draws the conclusions that if he waits a bit he won't need a raincoat and umbrella to go downtown. Here we have an empirical evaluation, on the basis of a sampling of direct observations plus some prior knowledge of the behavior of showers in that locale. The person might finish his coffee, then glance out again to confirm or negate his evaluation about a coming letup. If he's wrong, he'll either get soaked or needlessly carry around rainwear all day.

This quite ordinary inquiry contains all the basic elements of research, as summarized in Figure 2. We might add only the ethics of communicating results honestly. If a person told a blind man it wasn't raining, and the blind believer stepped forth only to get soaked, it would be a dishonor.

Figure 2 not only displays the basic elements common to both ordinary inquiry and professional research but it also conveys some sense of the important differences stemming from the higher standards imposed by respect for the rules of research and their wider scope of application. We will not now dwell on such differences, but they should never be far from mind in our examination of basic similarities.

The example in Figure 2 is an instance of the simplest research model—checking out one particular case or scene, noting its main features and perhaps some of the details, and making some tentative inference about what is found. Within social research, careful investigations of this type have produced some of the best ethnographies and investigative journalism pieces ever done. But this

FIGURE 2. Basic Elements of Inquiry and Research

Elements of Inquiry	Typical Inquirer	Professional Researcher
Questions	"Is it still raining? Is it going to rain all day?"	"What is the expected precipitation profile for the next 72 hours?"
Resources	Common-sense weather lore. Personal memory. Ordinary perceptual abilities.	Training in scientific meteorology. Decades of local weather records. Computers, weather satellites, worldwide network of observatories.
Sampling	What he can see from window. Personal experience with local weather.	Current weather data for the entire globe. Decades of local weather data.
Data	Subjective perceptions (what he can see, hear, feel, and smell).	Instrument readings (hygrometers, barometers, satellite pictures, radar, etc.).
Measurement	Subjective and crude assessments ("there's a damp breeze from the water; it's cooling off; it's lighter in the west").	Objective, precise, and accurate measurements (relative humidity, temperature gradient across the frontal boundary, etc.).
Analysis	Intuitive judgments ("the dark clouds seem to be moving away now").	Calculations (of dew point, ground speed of frontal movements, etc.).
Evaluation	"That's good enough for me; it simply can't rain on our picnic tonight".	Calculates specific probabilities of significant precipitation for this morning, this afternoon, and tonight.
Communication	"Tom, I think it will quit pretty soon. I'll pick you up at five for the picnic".	Worldwide public announcement of forecast by radio, TV, teletype.

elementary example can also illustrate some of the potential pitfalls awaiting the unwary investigator. Some local feature or temporary condition may be taken for the typical or the whole story. Our typical inquirer might, for instance, overgeneralize that it always rains in the morning, then clears; or that showers are always brief in that locale. Or, conversely, he might fail to make the valid generalization—that showers are almost always brief when lighter sky can be seen in the west—and miss the patterned regularity that exists.

MORE COMPLEX MODELS

A second research model, one step up in level of complexity, is the comparison of two things. The person in the street compares two products, or gets a second opinion; the researcher compares rural and urban life, or preliterate and modern communities. Here one is looking for similarities and differences, and perhaps also some clues as to why these occur. Exploring an unusual case is basically an implicit comparison with the usual or mainstream—for example, studying a child raised in isolation, or a community with no crime—and often leads to important breakthroughs, as we will later see. Comparison of one thing with another is as old as human history; the trained researcher is just more rigorous in his measurements and drawing of conclusions than is the rest of the populace.

One further step up in complexity is the exploration of a variable; that is, exploring the range of variation in something—life styles, responses to a new treatment, or attitudes toward a new President. A variable is any feature that can vary (in type or degree) from case to case. Other examples of variables would be height, age, amount of income, size of families, popularity, degree of proficiency in some skill, and so on. Virtually anything can be represented as a variable. We shall see in later chapters how professional researchers have gone about measuring and exploring these things called variables.

At this level the researcher usually becomes interested (one more step up) in some relationship between two variables, such as variations in attitude toward the new President by age, or male versus female opinions on the abortion issue. This is a classic research model, both in science and in life. Any relationship found (or not found) between two features may be only a description: "Older people are less favorable toward rock music than are younger people."

But at this still simple level, the investigator is usually looking for some "cause-effect" or "if, then" association between the variables that might provide more understanding, predictability and, perhaps, control of some area. Of course, many relationships are not of the straightforward cause-and-effect type, but show interdependence or feedback aspects. For instance, if you cheer someone up, he or she will usually feel better physically, and conversely, if you help someone feel better physically, he or she will usually be more cheerful. But most humans are looking for the "if you brush your teeth, it will reduce cavities" type of theorems. These are particularly sought by people in the business of applying findings. Will daily dosages of vitamin E reduce the incidence of heart trouble? Do stiffer prison sentences reduce crime rates? Does the Narcanon program reduce drug abuse? The basic question is, does the manipulation of one variable create an effect upon another variable? This is the kind of knowledge most sought after by both scientists and laymen so that they can do something to create some desired effect or effectively handle some undesirable condition.

Even when our inquiry into the relationship between two variables is only descriptive (such as the finding that average female life-spans are longer than male in most modern societies), such results can serve as a springboard for further studies to probe why the relationship occurs. Also, we can look into the wider circumstances under which the relationship holds true, and when it doesn't. (These wider circumstances are called *contextual variables*.) Thus mere descriptive findings can actually provide useful knowledge.

The relationship between two variables can be straightforward, or linear—the more A, the more B—but very often they are not. For example, a certain degree of stress may be invigorating both psychologically and physiologically, but past a certain point of increase, stress causes extreme physical and mental symptom patterns. The shape of a relationship can take virtually any geometric form.

So now we have variation in two characteristics and the relationship (if any) between them. It is often important to find no relationship; such findings can dispel myths and indicate dead ends so that investigators can turn elsewhere. If Scuffy facial treatment does nothing to clear up blemishes, we need to know that. The strength or degree of a relationship from none, to slight, to moderate, to strong, to total is just as important as its shape. The stronger a relationship, the greater is its value as a description, an explanation, a predictor, or a means of control.

Of course one can, and often does, investigate more than two variables in a study, in which case one examines all possible combinations of relationships among all the variables. Such multiple-variable inquiries lead into exploring the interrelationships among three or more variables, for instance, a breakdown of movie preferences by age, sex, and level of education. Modern computers have fantastically increased our ability to simultaneously analyze large numbers of variables and all the levels and patterns of relationships among them. But, lest we give all the credit to gadgetry, keen observers and creative artists have been doing this in a more qualitative way since the dawn of humanity.

Inquiry into a multitude of factors and the possible combinations among them is common, both in large research projects and in many life situations. Surveys, experiments, or field studies—as well as practical situations like evaluating a community for business opportunities or as a place to live—are likely to involve a large number of factors. Again, the major differences between the professional researcher and the ordinary human being are that the researcher carries out his inquiry by following explicit rules; and with these rules, he is less likely to commit the mistakes that potentially await any investigator. These two differences are crucial, for they have given us all the sciences.

BLUNDERS AND BLINDERS

The mistakes that can be made in attempting to find something out are probably endless in variety, and most of us have probably made all of them in one situation or another in our lives. Pitfalls encompass two broad categories—*blunders* (error) and *blinders* (bias)—which the successful investigator, whether scientist or layman, needs to avoid. The rules of social research exist, in good part, to minimize these risks.

Let us begin with blunders, or the problem of error. Often, people obtain too few data (of perhaps questionable validity), draw hasty conclusions, and act—sometimes to their sorrow. At the very least, they might have done much better. This is how, for example, many people make investments, buy major purchases, choose their careers, and select their mates. Bankruptcy, unemployment, and divorce rates partly reflect the results. Inappropriately formulated questions frame these inquiries, pursued through inadequate sampling that results from inadequate resources. Haphazard data gathering, inaccurate measurement, and makeshift analysis compound these errors, and overly casual evaluation efforts and a reluctance to communicate the nature and results of the inquiry to a critical public decrease the likelihood that any of these errors will be detected and corrected.

In terms of data, for example, many people accept hearsay and secondhand opinion as hard fact: "Kevin says it's a good investment" or "Sally says he's a good doctor to go to." The professional researcher may use hearsay for leads, as in field studies, but he does some kind of verifying or cross-checking before accepting it as factual.

Many people accept uncritically the advice of authorities. Authorities are useful to consult; they can be stimulating and maybe (but not necessarily) even right. When people know little about some subject, and know little about how to find out, they fall back on authorities. For the professional researcher, however, authority does not verify a premise. Science is notoriously irreverent toward authorities.

Asking friends or colleagues may provide useful first leads but has all the pitfalls mentioned plus a probable bias because of similar viewpoint and experience—one Communist asking another what's wrong with America. A professional researcher might get ideas from friends and colleagues but will run some strict empirical confirmation tests on them.

Being taken in by promotion and public relations claims, or propaganda, goes along the same line. These will not stand up to the rules of evidence in scientific research.

The list of possible mistakes could be lengthened indefinitely. There is desperation, which can lead a person to substitute wish for fact. There is a kind of self-deception where the person's convictions are so strong that he or she is impervious to any contrary environmental evidence. There is naiveté that leads one to plunge ahead with first impressions—leaping before really looking. And there is undue caution, stemming prehaps from long-standing habits or fixed thought patterns. History and daily life provide many examples of each of these pitfalls.

Perhaps the grandfather of all mistakes in human inquiry is overgeneralizing from the specific data at hand. One dating experience is not really sufficient to posit a beautiful relationship; a few successful results from a treatment are not sufficient to warrant wide release and announcement of a cure. But people continually form sweeping general conclusions from bits and pieces of preliminary data. The professional researcher is bound by more stringent guidelines in drawing conclusions and in generalizing from the data.

Two other mistakes within the element of analysis are rejecting a hypothesis because of insufficient evidence when it is actually true, and accepting a hypothesis as true because of strong evidence when it actually is false (Type I and Type II errors). An example of the first would be releasing a suspect when in fact he is guilty, and the second would be convicting someone who is actually innocent. Mystery dramas and social research alike are concerned with these paired risks; both the master detective and the professional researcher employ rigorous tests in treading the thin line between the two mistakes.

The second broad class of pitfalls in human inquiry is the large variety of *blinders*, or biases. Often we use persuasion to convince ourselves and others that we are correct, instead of honestly evaluating events. This is not necessarily a lack of integrity; the belief may serve some important psychological function for the person, so that it is too "costly" to let it go. This pitfall includes neglecting, or explaining away, any contrary evidence, instead of reevaluating a belief on the basis of the facts. It may even extend to include the active seeking of only confirming evidence and opinion. One might, for instance, look for supporting evidence that oil stocks are a good investment or that it would be good to have a relationship with Vinnie, *after* one has already decided. This is backwards research—going backwards from conclusion to evidence.

Another major source of potential bias in any social research, amateur or professional, is that it is carried out by live, opinionated social beings. There is probably no such thing as a totally detached and utterly objective researcher. Can a person do objective research on something he loves or hates? At a milder level, everyone has some sort of attitude toward virtually any subject that might be studied, and these attitudes produce an angle or slant from which we view situations.

The researcher is always an active agent in the research process.

Never does he or she passively go about finding out what is there. Even a photograph is taken from some angle (and not from many possible other angles), and it is given meaning by the human viewer.

One conceives, plans, and carries out any inquiry from a prior conceptual framework and set of perspectives. From these already existing perspectives one perceives, organizes the new perceptions, and concludes. These provide the angle from which the world is viewed and the starting points for the path of inquiry followed. They also somewhat predetermine the questions asked and, perhaps equally important, the questions never asked. There are physiological, psychological, sociological, and anthropological aspects of the researchers that influence the research done.

The communication systems of science are set up in part to overcome these potential biases by making possible replication, testing, verification, and refinement by others. But if all the colleagues share much the same culture and basic training, they may approach the environment with similar perspectives and thus share the same biases. The fact that a researcher is always an active agent in the research process means that he or she shapes as well as finds the results, and those from the same school will tend to exert similar influences upon their materials. For example, there is not much difference among the major television networks in their coverage of the evening news; but how different might the presentation of a Chinese, Dutch, or African commentator be of the same events? Their respective slants would diverge to a notable extent.

Each profession tends to develop its own approach to the world, organized along its own distinctive premises, that influences the practitioner's concepts and the questions he poses or never thinks to pose. For example, a physiologist might study cancer from a strict chemical/biological approach, a public health researcher with some social psychological training might pursue psychosomatic factors such as life crises, and a religious leader might seek some cleansing regimen and the alleviation of spiritual travails. Note that each would probably have great difficulty in communicating his perspective to the others.

These and similar biases can produce a kind of tunnel vision in which the researcher finds it hard to break loose from his own preconceptions and preoccupations to get broader or fresher perspectives on his or her subject matter. Just doing more research will not necessarily break the person loose when a fresh approach to the whole problem may be what is needed. If a person has worked on a problem too long, he or she may have little distance from it and hence little real objectivity.

The researcher often experiences some difficulty in rising above the approaches implicit and embedded in his or her native culture and professional training. Yet, we will see, especially in Chapter 15, that the rules of research have proved the most effective means yet found by humankind for doing so.

We have seen that research is the bridge between the empirical world and our mental conceptions of it. The flow across this bridge is always two-way, with the research materials influencing the inquirer and vice versa. Professional research strives by every means possible to make this flow as unblocked and free of extraneous influences as possible. Anything that blocks or diverts this two-way traffic is a hindrance to real knowledge.

This brief examination of blunders and blinders—errors and biases—begins to show something of how valuable the rules of professional research might be. The professional, of course, is not invulnerable to these common pitfalls, but the likelihood and seriousness of such mistakes are sharply reduced by following the established guidelines we will examine in later chapters.

After looking at all that can go wrong with an inquiry, one might begin to get the feeling that good research is impossible. Happily, this is not so. The quality of research is relative, and use of professional procedures will guarantee increased quality. Also, research is a collective thing; the whole international research community keeps this wheel of collective human intelligence rolling along to an ever-increasing understanding of the universe around us.

PART
II

ELEMENTS OF
RESEARCH

Even the most complex and elaborate research revolves around a few key elements that can be easily grasped and permit searching analysis of the relative merits of any inquiry, in any field, under any circumstances.

Human inquiry, after all, is a process of working up an answer to some question, and can be compared with other productive human enterprises. For example, the key elements of inquiry introduced in Chapter 2 have their counterparts in the art of cooking.*

A research question (Chapter 3) can be likened to the cook's idea of what he wants to produce—perhaps inspired by a scrumptious color photo of some dish in a homemaker's magazine. Resources (Chapter 4) are just as important in research as in cooking; does the cook have, or can he or she afford to obtain, the necessary ingredients, tools, kitchen facilities, time, knowledge, and experience required to cook up this dish? Sampling (Chapter 5) corresponds to the cook's need to shop around for and attempt to locate the best possible appropriate ingredients—in the researchers' case, data. Data collection (Chapter 6) corresponds to the cook's selecting, substituting, and preparing the raw ingredients. Measurement (Chapter 7) is as important in research as in cooking;

---

*Our comparison of research with cooking—a recurrent theme through the remainder of the book—was inspired by (but differs from) the formulation of John B. Williamson, David A. Karp, John R. Dalphin, and Paul S. Gray, *The Research Craft: An Introduction to Social Research Methods*, 2nd ed. (Boston: Little, Brown, 1982), pp. 36–62.

inaccurate measurement can easily spoil the broth. Analysis of data (Chapter 8) corresponds to blending and cooking the ingredients. Evaluation (Chapter 9) is an ongoing quality-control process; the cook carefully scrutinizes the ingredients, monitors the degree of their blending, and how far along the cooking has progressed, perhaps testing with a toothpick to see how well done and, ultimately, invoking the taste test. Communication (Chapter 10) involves not only passing on the eventual product—serving the dish and receiving critical reviews—but reading recipe books, articles, and books on cooking, proposing menus to the family, and talking to oneself and one's helpers throughout the process.

But do not be misled by the order of listing of these elements. The process of human inquiry is no more linear than the process of cooking. The process may begin with practically any one of these elements. The cook may not begin with an idea of what to cook; perhaps a neighbor gives us a bag of fresh tomatoes or a couple of fish, or we receive a new cooking tool for Christmas, and then we cast about for what we might want to make with these. Similarly, in research, one might stumble upon an unusual sampling opportunity or an unanticipated data set or a new technique for measurement or analysis. Only then does the researcher begin to figure

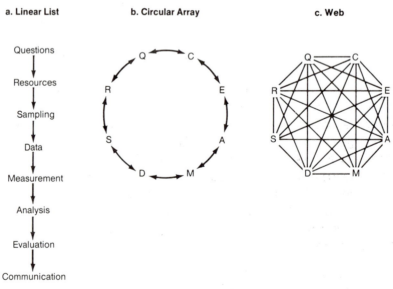

FIGURE 3. Models of Relations Among Basic Elements of Research

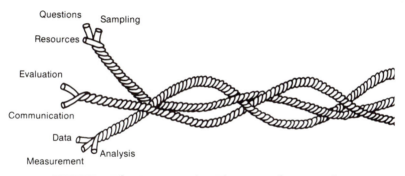

FIGURE 4. The Interweaving Elements of Research

out an appropriate research question. The elements of research constitute not so much a linearly ordered list (see a. in Figure 3) , but rather a circular array that can be entered at any point (see b. in Figure 3). The researcher does not travel around that circle but shuttles back and forth across the circle, weaving a dense web of trails linking all eight of the elements (c. in Figure 3).

As a result, the eight elements are not separate and discrete but are interweaving and mutually supportive, like the several cords comprising a rope, the "lifeline of inquiry" (Figure 4) on which we all depend. The strength of this lifeline depends not only on the strength of each element but also on the way they are all interwoven. Like a lifeline, any inquiry has a beginning and an end. At any point along the line, one element may loom larger or more prominent than others, but a close inspection at that point will reveal that all the others are still there as continuous and reinforcing threads from beginning to end. Inquiry is never a fixed sequence of discrete steps but is always a progressive intertwining of basic elements.

CHAPTER
3
QUESTIONS

The similarity between the words *quest* and *question* is not accidental. Each involves a search of some sort and something unknown. Any inquiry of any kind involves some implicit or explicit questions that remind us what it is we are trying to find out. Even a simple interest or curiosity about something is a vague, unfocused, unformulated question.

Everyone continually poses a lot of questions in their personal lives, in their work, and in their idle curiosities about themselves and the world around them. The questions posed by researchers simply have some special qualities. For one thing, researchers try to pose questions that can be empirically answered. As individuals we might ask, "What is the meaning of life?" but we would not tackle this on our next research project. We might, however, research the meanings that people assign to their lives. A question must be *answerable* within the framework and resources of the project.

Questions that are too general or vague may serve as starting points in thinking about some subject area, but they will not do for the actual research. For example, a question such as, "How do older and younger people differ in their attitudes toward life?" must be broken down into specific attitude questions and specific age categories (say, over forty and under forty). More specific questions lead to more precise data gathering and to more precise and usable conclusions.

Professional research also demands unbiased or nonloaded questions. "Why are men better than women?" is a loaded question, acceptable perhaps for barbershop banter but not in an investigation, because it already presupposes male superiority. Researchers attempt to be as objective as possible in the questions they pose. Some questions might flow naturally and sensibly from a particular culture and belief system but be unacceptable for empirical research. "Will the gods bless our fishing today?" may seem a perfectly sound and legitimate question to members of one culture but rank as sheer superstition to members of a different culture. In its striving for objectivity, professional research tries to rise above such cultural biases in questions. This is a major means through which the professional seeks to overcome the blinders of his or her culture, training, and personal convictions.

Research also seeks questions that are useful—theoretically, practically, or both. For instance, finding out how decisions are actually made in organizations would probably be more important than finding out which types of plastic cups are preferred at the water cooler. Questions that are crucial to some theory are particularly valuable, but so are questions important to some practical concern. Judging the usefulness of questions is tricky for two reasons. First, such judgments depend on one's perspective; to the supply officer of a large company, the plastic cups question could well seem the more important. Second, the seemingly most trivial questions have sometimes proved to have enormous impact upon both the history of ideas and the history of the world. Nevertheless, the judged importance or usefulness of a question must be given some consideration, because the resources for research are always limited.

Often research involves a *progression* of questions, perhaps beginning with a vague inquisitiveness. For many people, this may be about as far as it goes; a vague answer is found and the person lets it go at that: "it's human nature," or "our money is safe at Snafu Savings." The professional researcher instead goes on to wonder more explicitly and to frame questions that are specific, empirically answerable, objective, and relevant to his or her interests. These are some of the first rules of the research game.

SCREENING FOR OBJECTIVITY AND RELEVANCE

The relevance and objectivity of research questions are not so readily assured as they might at first seem. In fact, scientists often spend a great deal of time and effort working out their specific research questions. The questions pursued in professional research do not always derive from impersonal and well-developed scientific theories, as many accounts of research imply. Even in professional research, the sources of questions are legion: previous research (either particular studies or empirical generalizations), cultural stereotypes and popular conceptions, some deep personal concern of the researcher, the practical needs and interests of others, political concerns, and the topical priorities of those who fund research. Often, then, the original questions that give rise (and, sometimes, resources) to the investigation have a slant or bias of some sort that must be screened out if the inquiry is to be objective. Also, the original quest of those who are providing resources may be trivial—for our wheel of collective human understanding and for the best interests of the providers. For instance, a commercial company may set out to prove its product is best and only wish their researchers to provide "findings" that confirm this position. This approach is likely to yield statistics that lie, cheat, and steal.

Because many research questions are externally derived (if not imposed), it is most important that the researcher clarify the nature of any question to assure that it is sufficiently objective, specific, and empirically answerable. Some burning public concern, or some medical situation, or manufacturing problem that may obtain easy research funding does not automatically translate into the basic questions that will help resolve the problem. Here, the art of posing research questions that lead to useful answers comes into full play.

Posing questions that are empirically answerable is also not as simple as it might at first seem. We do not have a clear question until we know what replies would count as direct answers. Not every sensible reply to a question is an answer; for example, in response to the question "What's a good way to predict how a relationship will turn out?", the well-intended and perhaps helpful replies "There isn't any," "You'll find one in this book," or "That's a good question" are not *answers* to the question asked. Even such a seemingly specific question as "Who is that man living next door?" is not immediately answerable because it is difficult to anticipate just what kind of answer would satisfy the questioner. Does he want a proper name, or some kind of description? If the latter, is it one involving where he's from, what he does for a living, a thumbnail sketch of his character, or what? Often the questioner doesn't really know what he wants, but after our best-guess reply he may tell us if that reply relieved his (apparently vague) puzzlement, and perhaps he may then be led to ask a clearer question that will better satisfy his quest. If you listen awhile to ordinary conversations, you will notice that they are filled with responses to questions that are not really answers.

It is for these reasons that many interesting but vague questions—"What is the relation between thought and language?" or "Why are there so many species of insects?" or "How do children learn language?"—are not genuine research questions. We do not really know what would count as possible direct answers. Therefore, questions such as these might provide jumping-off points for inquiry, but we would then go on to frame questions we could directly answer with our available research tools: "If we increase someone's vocabulary, does he score better on problem-solving tests?" "Does ordinary earth radiation produce mutations resulting in insect species which survive?" "At what age do infants first repetitively use a specific sound to denote some particular object?"

One often must struggle a bit in translating some broad research interest into questions that are specifically and clearly answerable within the scope of an investigation, given always limited resources. "Where shall we live?" must somewhere along the line become something like "Shall we move to Dallas?" "What's a cure for the common cold?" must be broken down into such queries as "Do rapid temperature changes increase the incidence of colds?" and "Do daily doses of 1,000 milligrams of vitamin C significantly reduce the number of colds caught per thousand population over a one-year time span?"

But, of course, many questions that are quite clear are still not good research questions. "How many angels can dance on the head of a pin?" As the saying goes, ask a foolish question and you get a foolish answer. Many clear questions are really still only speculative at this time. How might silicon-based life forms reproduce? What significant differences are there in the political attitudes of people 200 years old versus those of people 100 years old? Would life on a planet with less gravity significantly affect divorce rates over a ten-year period for a matched group of young marrieds? Such questions could be refined to the point where they were superb research hypotheses except that we could not answer them directly because we have no way to do the investigating. Also, a biased question slants toward only some of the alternative direct answers. This is in fact a rather good definition of bias—a slanting of the alternative direct answers to the question. "When did John stop beating his wife?" is so loaded that whatever the direct answer, he comes off as a nerd.

A good research question must be not only definitely answerable but must be *empirically* answerable. We do not deny that truths can sometimes be reached in other ways: logic, lucky guesses, plausible reasoning, intuition, perhaps even spiritual awareness. But a good research question is one that must be answered by determining empirical facts. Although the answer found in a particular study may not always be a true answer (because we failed to properly determine the facts), we can all agree on the type of procedure necessary to answer the question by referring to our standard research guidelines.

TYPES OF QUESTIONS

The kinds of questions posed will heavily influence the type of investigation that follows. We want the questions to focus and guide the research without throttling it. The majority of projects do go beyond the questions posed, and surprises turn up not infrequently that lead to new questions. A study of muggings, for instance, indicates widespread agreement among muggers on just who to accost and who to leave alone in a stream of foot traffic. This then leads to questions about what characteristics mark pedestrians as prone to mugging or not. Any good study always raises as many questions as it answers and thus carries our wheel of collective human knowledge forward. But even so, the initial questions always set the framework for what follows.

The various forms that research can take differ mainly in the type of research question that each seeks to answer, as we shall see in Part III. Even the three fundamental purposes of research—description, explanation, and verification—pose quite different classes of questions. Everyday speech is filled with queries that reflect these three classes: "what is it?" (description), "how does it work?" (explanation), and "is it true?" (verification).

Description basically involves "what's going on here?" kinds of questions. Descriptive research is also often called exploratory research, but even here it is best to have some focus for organizing the looking into. Even description requires specific, objective, and empirically answerable questions. In one way or another, descriptive questions usually ask who, which, what, when, where, how often, or how many. The form these elementary questions take will vary somewhat between different models of research; for example, within the model of exploring the variation in a variable (such as body type), we will want to know how many variations there are, what these are, and how often each occurs. One step up, in examining the relationship between two variables, we will want to ask the strength, shape, and direction of that relationship. Because descriptive or exploratory research tends to be directed toward some lesser known aspect of an area, it is quite common for such research to uncover answers that are unexpected, puzzling, or even surprising, giving rise to further questions. These types of research are also often called pilot studies.

The purpose of explanatory research is to answer questions of the "how come?" variety. We are seeking the *reasons* for certain facts or events. Explanation is the backbone not only of scientific research but also of investigations in applied fields, from medicine to financial planning to police work. In both theoretical and practical work, one seeks explanations for their own sake perhaps, but also usually with the intent to predict and control events in some area. Explanatory questions are particularly difficult to frame satisfactorily, because to ask for an explanation is to ask for information that would fill in some critical gap in the questioner's understanding of how things happen. What would count as an explanation depends entirely on what the questioner thinks he already knows; thus, the same explanation that is perfectly satisfying to one person may be almost totally irrelevant and unsatisfying to another. It is for such reasons that explanatory research tends to be favorably received by others who share a single approach (on the basis of a common culture and training) but is often viewed somewhat skeptically by investigators in other professions and other countries. But we have the means for rising above such squabbles.

Explanations will stand up when they lead to correct predictions (or understandings) of events and when they can be *verified.* When we can predict and verify that tooth brushing with a fluoride paste will significantly reduce the number of cavities per hundred children per year, we can safely feel that we are getting somewhere.

Verification (or hypothesis testing) studies are framed in response to questions of the "is it really so?" variety. Even small children are notoriously curious about questions of this sort and constantly undertake verification inquiries to test the truth of what they have been told. Mother has said a hundred times that the stove is hot, but is it really so? Whereas children generally seek simple yes-no answers, professional researchers seldom envision simple answers but ask "is it always true that ... " or "when is it true that ... " In research, as in daily life, an untested idea usually needs some sort of confirmation before it is acted on, in order to ensure some success and to avoid possible unpleasant consequences.

As you would suppose, research on a given topic often follows a progression from descriptive questions to explanatory questions to verification questions. Each represents a rough stage in our increasing understanding of some area. For example, in examining government statistics we might note the odd descriptive fact that married men outlive single men on the average, but single women tend to outlive married women. One might investigate this by seeking an explanation in unbalanced privileges and responsibilities of male and female sex roles, or the alleviating influence of outside activities. One might then go on to verify an explanation, perhaps finding it true only under certain circumstances.

A sense of having found something out hinges, in the end, on a feeling that one has answered some kind of question—vague or specific, theoretical or practical, conceptual or empirical. Research is an attempt to answer questions that are, by the rules of the game, well-formulated questions. How good an answer a researcher can find is determined in good part by his or her resources, the topic to which we now turn.

CHAPTER

4

RESOURCES

An important element of any research enterprise is the *resources* one has or can find for pursuing it. Resources are not often talked about in research courses or texts, but they are a real fact of life in any kind of inquiry. There is a close and special relationship between the words *invest* and *investigate*. Knowledge always entails some costs, at least in personal time and effort, and producing it always requires investment of resources that are never limitless and are often scarce.

However, the relationship between resources available and research done is not a hard and fast one. Vast resources of money, facilities, and personnel do not necessarily produce good investigation or discovery. Neither do scant resources preclude major successes or scientific breakthroughs. Even in the physical sciences, a good many major achievements have been produced by those with quite modest resources.

Resources are any and all factors a person can marshal to utilize in the pursuit of some particular inquiry. But resources are not passive, for they can be discovered, created, or extended by the canny inquirer. This is why some people are called *resourceful*.

So what is the relationship between resources and finding out? First of all, available resources inevitably set limits on the *scope* of any investigation. A shopper can't look forever for the best buy; a pollster can't interview everyone in America; an anthropologist can't examine every single detail of a tribe. *Sampling* is a major answer that professional researchers have developed to resolve these problems of scope limitations, as discussed in Chapter 5. Yet, the scope of samples is largely determined by the resources at hand.

Second, available resources channel and facilitate the *directions* a study takes. For instance, suppose one is interested in ethnic assimilation; if one is living in Alaska, he or she is then likely to study the Eskimos, but if in Texas, one would probably study Mexican immigrants. Particular resources provide particular opportunities for particular directions of inquiry. Distinctive resources make possible and encourage the investigation of distinctive topics and rule out others. At the same time, resources influence *how* any particular topic will be investigated; if a medical laboratory has only X-ray equipment, it will study tumors through X-ray techniques rather than through, say, CAT-scan techniques.

Third, the flip side of any resource is a constraint. Although a given resource makes possible and facilitates certain directions of research, it also limits the directions a study might take. An optical telescope may direct our research toward the stars, but it will constrain the kinds of questions we ask—for example, preventing us from addressing questions that those who have radio telescopes can effectively pursue.

If we increase our understanding of what resources are, we can learn to stretch the limits they impose and to take advantage of the opportunities they provide. The acquiring of resources is part of the research game.

MATERIAL RESOURCES

Material resources, such as time, money, facilities, and personnel, are perhaps the most obvious things that affect the scope and direction of any investigation. Of these, time is often the most limited resource, both in daily life and in science. As a great teacher used to tell his classes, if someone works long enough in an area he is bound to come up with something. But often, one doesn't have a long enough time for that slow accumulation of sifted observations and pyramiding knowledge; the time one can spend on an inquiry is never endless.

To get more of an idea of the impacts of these material resources, consider two contrasting situations, each of which is fairly typical. In the first, an investigator is willing to devote most of his career to a single project but has practically no money, facilities, or support personnel. In the second, the government makes available huge amounts of material resources but must have the research question answered immediately.

The penniless investigator must pursue his study like a (perhaps obsessive) hobby, taking advantage over the years of whatever opportunities he can find. He cannot afford to be too fussy about preferred directions or the scope of his data, but he can examine with unrivaled care and thoroughness what data he obtains. Moreover, he can afford to examine how these data change over time—asking longitudinal or process questions. Also, he can pick up data and ideas from related fields, and he can ponder over the bits and pieces as one might work a grand puzzle.

The mammoth crash project, on the other hand, is a large-scale bureaucratic enterprise, often beset by internal disputes over the proper formulation of the research questions and over the best methods and techniques to employ. The scope of data collection is often awesome, but the pressures of deadlines typically rule out longitudinal questions and ensure that analysis of these data will be incomplete and selective. The expensive equipment and facilities are used for only a short time, and the highly select personnel are soon let go, their special training a spent resource.

Both of these situations have produced results that have increased knowledge in every field. But you can readily see the weaknesses of each, and you can see how some combination of the two would be more nearly optimal.

HUMAN RESOURCES

Human resources, including the knowledge, skills, and dedication of the researchers, may be less tangible than the count of personnel, equipment, and budget, but may in the end be more important. It is here that the skilled researcher, even the penniless investigator, can hope to surmount material limitations.

Knowledge begets knowledge; the prior knowledge level of the researcher is probably the crucial resource and the most effective investment in any investigation. All the legendary wealth of the Inca's empire could not manage to buy him answers to questions about nutrition or space travel, because the imperial wise men of that realm did not yet have a general prior knowledge level sufficient to properly formulate those questions or to perceive and appreciate the significant clues. Conversely, an investigator with a great deal of prior knowledge in some area might need to do only a little research to find out much more. The extent to which the inquirer knows his craft, coupled with his degree of ingenuity, seems to be the major variable determining how far he gets.

Knowledge is not merely a mass of raw information. Knowledge is organized information—organized by concepts, ideas, theories, and principles into some sort of coherent conceptual framework. Without appropriately powerful concepts and principles, any investigator would soon be swamped by tides of unorganized information. For instance, the ordinary person walking into a medical laboratory is utterly bewildered and overwhelmed by the welter of machines and gadgets, but the lab technician—because he or she has mental concepts that fit with all these items—perceives simply a set of tools. Prior knowledge thus bounds the scope of investigation. These same organizing concepts and principles provide the basis for the investigator's questions and guide their formulation; knowledge of a given subject matter makes possible and encourages distinctive directions of research. Any specific inquiry rests upon where our wheel of collective human intelligence has gotten to. And it further rests on the investigator's knowing the current level of understanding. The knowledge level of the inquirer is crucial in determining what is actually found out.

The blinders discussed in Chapter 2 may limit and constrain this process of accumulating wisdom; a professional can become set in his ways and locked in, operating from unexamined premises and approaches so that there are fruitful questions he or she will never ask. However, there are safeguards against this possibility, as we will see in Chapter 15, and the research game is played in such a way that someone else will probably come along and pose the telling new questions.

Personal traits of the researcher are also important influences. Psychological studies on the character of scientists, for example, find not only imaginativeness and a willingness to take risks but also the countervailing traits of self-discipline and dedication. The successful researcher is, more often than not, one who has done a great deal of homework and who has put in more than a minimal nine-to-five effort. The dedication and perseverance of accomplished researchers are legendary; Edison would not sleep but only napped at his laboratory bench and, through incredible persistence, produced a practical light bulb on which others had given up. The resources of dedication and persistance substantially affect the scope of any inquiry, and imaginativeness and discipline together influence the quality of that effort.

The researcher's personal abilities and skills are also important influences on the directions and manner of investigation. A sightless researcher will not choose observational methods and a severe stutterer may avoid the use of interview methods; someone highly skilled in the design and analysis of experiments will not be too interested in pursuing a topic or question that seems to require survey research.

Even such demographic characteristics of the researcher as age, sex, and race can be assets or liabilities, encouraging certain directions of research and discouraging others. A female may find it difficult or personally distasteful to carry on research in prisons or the military, and a white investigator may find that he has limited success in studying the street life of black youths.

ENVIRONMENTAL RESOURCES

Environmental resources must also be taken into account. For example, the answers to a great many vital research questions no doubt already exist, lying around in bits and pieces in the libraries and archives of mankind, just waiting for a bright young inquirer to fit them together. As pointed out in Chapter 2, access to many decades of local weather data is one important factor that makes the professional meteorologist more successful in forecasting than the man in the street. Available impersonal information is such a vital resource that its use is a mode of research in its own right, as discussed in Chapter 11. What existing information and how much is available can influence the scope of investigation as well as its directions and manner.

Access to existing information has always been an important resource in human history. Modern printing and mass communications have greatly increased both the spread and the accumulation of information. This acceleration can be seen in various estimates that knowledge has increased as much in our own lifetime as in all the previous history of the human race. As we come into the postindustrial information society, this resource becomes all the more crucial in theoretical, practical, and personal matters, as we will see.

INFLUENCE OF POLITICAL AND MORAL CLIMATES

Freedom of inquiry is an environmental condition that must not be overlooked. An open society that tolerates questions is a precious resource that too few of us properly appreciate. But even in a democratic and libertarian society, freedom of inquiry is not unbounded. The political climate and often the religious and the moral climates influence the research that can be done and how it can be carried out, and may even influence the types of questions it is safe to pose. In every time and place some topics, approaches, questions, and techniques are regarded as taboo and unsavory, even though these shady areas might contain vital answers. And on the other side, as we have seen in Chapter 3, the political climate may positively pressure researchers to pursue certain questions.

Although a moral climate might tolerate or even favor open inquiry it always imposes moral obligations on the researcher. The ethics of research are at once a human resource and an environmental resource, constraining the researcher to avoid, for example, experiments that cause pain to animals or that might alter people's personalities for the worse. Particularly within social research, the people studied may be betrayed, directly or indirectly. The researcher needs to be sensitive to unintended possible consequences of not only the research itself but also the communication of its results.

Even though human resources and environmental resources may be more critical than material resources, money is still the most liquid resource, in that any of the other resources can be bought with money. Money can buy facilities, helping hands, and even (in one sense) time. Because money can buy personnel, it can buy necessary knowledge, skills, and demographic characteristics by the hiring of personnel with the desired attributes. Money can also buy access to available archival information and can sometimes even buy freedom of inquiry. For instance, how much a government agency can find out about someone depends largely on how much it is willing to spend. And huge government funding, in large part, turned scattered theoretical equations into the atomic bomb. For all these reasons, money is a most useful resource for any investigation.

But it is neither an all-powerful resource nor an unmixed blessing. Money can buy only what is now or could reasonably be made available in the marketplace. Time, for example, can be bought only in the form of man-hours of effort, not in the form of calendar time. No matter how many dollars we earthlings might offer the gods, a solar eclipse cannot be delayed or extended for purposes of research. Similarly, only existing knowledge can be bought, as the Inca emperor learned to his sorrow. Even the purchase of equipment is subject to the same limitation; we cannot now buy a spaceship that will travel at the speed of light. And if we need to hire 200 Eskimos who speak Turkish and are adept in calculus, we may be in trouble, at least for the moment. Nor can money buy new answers if all share the same tunnel-vision predisposition toward the subject.

Moreover, money or the getting of money for research can sometimes be more trouble than it is worth. Often, money comes with influential strings attached; he who pays the piper calls the tune. The resource of money is often obtained at some cost against the alternative resource of freedom of inquiry.

IMPORTANCE OF ORGANIZATIONAL SKILLS

The organization of resources can also be thought of as a master resource making up for deficiencies in available resources. For example, organizational skills, such as cooperation, persuasion, and exchange, can often substitute for money. If I can't afford to go to Samoa to collect certain data, can I talk someone there into collecting them for me? If I'm good at interviewing and you're good at statistics, how about collaborating? In other ways, too, skillful coordination and management of available resources is a vital factor in the research enterprise. One can have a healthy budget, the finest facilities, and the best personnel but yet fail to launch a reasonable study because of poor organizational skills. If nothing else, one must efficiently budget his or her own time and effort, so there is a factor of efficiency in any inquiry. The management of personnel is typically the most difficult and challenging aspect of proper organization of resources; determining who should do what, when, and where and getting them to do so are fine arts. The importance of organizational skill is shown by the fact that many successful investigators have accomplished much through clever use of very meager resources.

Any enterprise of finding out is limited, channeled, and constrained by the available resources of the investigators. Sometimes one is able to find answers to one's questions quickly and easily, so that one's resource limits are never reached or tested, but this is not typical.

The discovery and utilization of resources are arts in which anyone can improve skills. One's environment actually abounds with potential resources for virtually any inquiry, as Darwin, Benjamin Franklin, and many others have demonstrated. With eyes to make observations, a voice to ask questions, some pens and paper to record findings, anyone can be an inquirer.

CHAPTER

5

SAMPLING

Most people are rather mystified about the subject of sampling. How can entire national elections be accurately predicted on the basis of a relative handful of early returns? How can a great deal about an alien planet be figured out from chemical tests on a few cubic centimeters of surface material? The ability to tell something about a whole slice of our environment from a few tiny bits seems nothing short of miraculous.

Yet, every human being continuously uses rudimentary sampling technology in every aspect of their daily lives. We sample the cooking at a new restaurant, sample interactions with a new relationship, sample service at a bank. A shopper samples prices and quality at different supermarkets. We sample the water before we jump in, and we are presented with a packaged sample of world events on the evening news. A biography samples some person's life. We are ever seeking to know the whole of something by knowing something about a bit of it.

This aspiration is the hallmark of intelligence. Intelligence, you'll recall, means learning from experience with the environment. Because the environment is a very large place, our experience of it is necessarily limited and selective. In seeking to understand the world, we can only reason from our small and peculiar sample of experiences with that world. And so we do, with generally good success.

But we all continually make *sampling errors*. Our sampling is often too limited; for instance, just trying a couple of stores, or marrying a person after half a dozen dates. Or we don't sample widely enough; we get our second medical opinion from a doctor just down the hall in the same clinic. Or our sampling is grossly unrepresentative; we investigate a school by talking with only its dropouts, or an organization by interviewing only its dedicated executives.

These mistakes occur because we tend to carry over into deliberate inquiry certain habits and skills developed in very different human activities. Sampling for purposes of finding out is a rather different business than sampling for other purposes. Consider, for example, sampling the large array of tomatoes at the supermarket. Our usual purpose in rummaging through this array is to find some perfectly ripe tomatoes or a few nice sized ones. We are interested in finding six that are good enough; we are usually not much interested in the lot as a whole, so it doesn't much matter if we're too short to reach the back rows or have the time to examine only the top layer. But the sellers of produce, on the other hand, are necessarily concerned with the entire lot: "Is this lot ripe enough to sell?" or "What's the size grade of these tomatoes?" In answering these questions so as to put the best price on the tomatoes, the seller cannot afford to look at just a few in the first row, as the shopper can. As we make our way through life, our experience is mostly in this shopper role, trying to do well enough with the environment rather than trying to learn the whole truth. As a result, when we deliberately seek to find something out, our shopper habits in sampling tend to carry over.

Also, in real life situations, there is often some urgency or desperation in our samplings. For example, if we need sudden medical attention, we cannot afford to coolly sample clinics in the area. And if we're in a rush to pick up ice and mix for a party, we are not likely to sample comparative store prices throughout the district. So, in our personal lives, circumstances often force expediency sampling upon us.

SAMPLING ERRORS

Sampling errors, accidental or deliberate, are a major source of false pictures in our daily lives. For example, reporting only the bad news from some geographic area will give outsiders a bad impression of that area. Lobbyists for urban renewal monies will display photos of run-down buildings, but real estate agents will display only beautiful sunny shots. Legions of workers are engaged in the business of manipulating the images that people accept as a true sampling of realities, so we would all do well to develop some canniness and sophistication on the subject of sampling.

The central role that sampling plays in inquiry is highlighted by the fact that the Latin roots of the word *intelligence* mean "to gather, pick, or choose among." These root meanings, in turn, should remind us that there are two fundamentally different sampling situations that may confront any inquiry: scarcity of cases, or abundance. The scarcity situation is the gathering type, in which the investigator must actively seek out and locate cases of the sort he wants to study. It may be difficult to find a full range of cases, or the inquirer may be seeking unusual cases such as children raised in isolation, people who have spontaneously regenerated body parts, or identical twins raised apart. Sampling then amounts to a process of case finding. The abundance situation is the picking and choosing type, in which the investigator has more possibilities than he or she can handle. Sampling then amounts to a process of case selection. The techniques of sampling are more fully developed for problems of case selection than for problems of case finding. This must not be taken to mean that one is more important than the other, and we will try to keep both situations in mind. Through our examination of them, you will see that case finding and case selection processes rest on the same basic premises.

The essential aim in any kind of sampling to answer a question is to get the same answer from study of the sample cases that we would have had we studied every existing case, that is, the population of cases. Obviously, it is the latter answer that really matters; the degree to which a sample-based answer diverges from a population-based answer is the measure of the degree of sampling error in any study.

But we are creatures of finite resources. Our experiences of the world are necessarily limited and selective. How can we presume that our small and peculiar samples could yield correct answers, without substantial sampling error? Once again, the rules and routines of professional research provide help.

Consider first the problem of limited experience. If the population of cases were completely homogeneous—that is, each case exactly identical to every other case—the size of a sample would not matter in the least. A sample consisting of even one case would yield the same answer as a study of all the cases. The more heterogeneous (varied) the population of cases, the more likely any single case is to be atypical and not representative of the whole lot. Heterogeneity has two aspects: the number of distinct types of cases, and the relative frequency of these types. Age in the American populace, for example, ranges from just born to over 110 years old, but sex is pretty well handled by two categories—male and female. The more categories, the less likely that any single case will be typical. The number of cases that fall into each category also affects sampling. If in a small sample we had no people over age 110, we wouldn't be too worried because there are very few of these in the population. But if we had no people between ages twenty and thirty, we'd know we were in trouble with our sampling.

How large must a sample be if we are not to be misled? Later in this chapter, we will discuss some techniques for deciding this question under specific circumstances. For now, let us remind you that larger samples are safer than smaller samples, everything else being equal, and that the more heterogeneous the population of cases, the larger the sample we will need to be safe. But be assured that adequate samples are very much within the bounds of human capabilities; for example, even a few hundred properly selected cases can quite precisely approximate the results of a complete census of American citizens. It is in this respect that sampling is the major strategy for coping with resource limitations.

Sheer numbers of cases are seldom the answer to a sampling problem. A sample of one, fifty, or a million must be meaningful in terms of what we want to find out. That is, it must provide a sufficiently sound data base for the purposes of the investigation. For instance, if we wanted to explore the populace's responses to a new presidential program, it would be better to sample twenty people from different walks of life than to sample 1,000 college students. Or, three contrasting stores would give a better basis for comparison shopping than ten stores all in the same chain.

We are thus brought around to the second, and more serious, problem of selective experience. If any sample-based answer to a research question is to yield the same answer as would a study of the entire population of cases, our sampling cannot be seriously selective. If any type of case that exists in the population is unrepresented in our sample, our sample is biased and is less likely to give us right answers. For example, if in studying American voters our sample contained no persons over age sixty, we would be seriously misled by our sample-based results. But selectivity also has a second face. Even though we might have avoided sample bias (by making sure all age categories of voters were included in our sample), the sample may be unrepresentative if the various types are not included in the same proportions in which they occur in the population. For example, if 25 percent of the voter population is actually over age sixty but our sample contained only 5 percent over age sixty, our final result would be significantly misleading, no matter how good our data gathering and analysis were. See Figure 5.

So, to obtain a sound sample, we must understand something of the shape of the population we want to sample. We need to know the types of cases that exist, so that we can represent them all, and we need to know something about their relative frequencies, so that we can represent them proportionately. The rub is that if we already know that much about the population, we would probably already have the answer to our research question and wouldn't need to bother studying a sample of cases. That is, in order to overcome completely the problems of bias and unrepresentativeness, we would need to know all the types and the frequency with which each occurs. But in real life or real science, we never do know that much about any population of interest; we never completely solve the problems of selectivity. Instead, we strive to reduce or minimize these problems by an informed, best-guess understanding of the shape of that slice of reality we wish to study. Quite often we do very well in such "guesstimates." As our knowledge of some particular area increases, our knowledge of the shape of its populations improves and, hence, our samplings tend to become better.

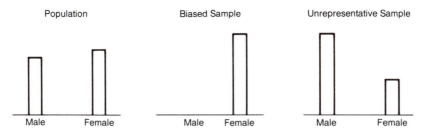

FIGURE 5. Bias and Unrepresentativeness of Samples.

STEPS IN SAMPLING PLAN

The key to the greater success of the professional investigator in sampling is his or her conscious formulation of an explicit, formal plan to improve the accuracy and efficiency of sampling within a given study. There are several steps in this formulation of a sampling plan.

The first step is to conceptualize the universe of cases that is appropriate to the research question; that is, to think through carefully what kinds of cases the question really pertains to. For example, the research question may concern determining American public opinion on some issue. Would we be interested in the views of all American citizens or only in those of registered voters? If citizens, should this include teenagers, young children, the legally insane, incarcerated criminals, and the like? Careful decisions must be made in drawing the boundaries of the relevant universe. If not, there may be a whole live area not included in the sample—for instance, the underground economy, or the world of unregistered migrant persons—that we entirely miss.

The second step is to learn as much as one can about the shape of the population of existing cases that fall within the boundaries of the conceptualized universe. About how many cases might there be altogether? What are the various types of cases, or subpopulations, that are known or might reasonably be expected to occur? What is our best information about their relative proportions? Here, too, the resource of prior knowledge comes into play, influencing the accuracy of one's rough understanding of the shape of the population. Pilot studies are particularly useful at this stage.

The third step is to formulate some sampling frame—a list, map, or plan of search that actually or potentially identifies in a practical way all the cases in the designated population. A sampling frame is rather straightforward in the case selection type of sampling; a sampling frame is a literal or figurative list of all the cases, from which a subset of cases will be drawn. In the case finding situation, a sampling frame is more like a list of sources that might each be able to provide a limited list of cases.

The fourth step is to select a sampling method—some specific procedure for using the sampling frame in case selection or case finding. The natural tendency of all human beings is to rely on convenience or haphazard methods, choosing those cases that are closest to hand (or to mind) or simply picking willy-nilly. These methods are almost guaranteed to result in samples that are both biased and unrepresentative. A close cousin is the cluster sampling method, picking, say, one city block or one hospital and interviewing all those persons who are found there. The justification is one of resource limitations; it is much cheaper to do many interviews at one site than to do one each at many scattered sites, but the problem is that any such cluster tends to be quite homogeneous in comparison with the population, leading again to biased and unrepresentative samples. A second cousin is the judgmental sampling method, in which one scans the sampling frame and picks cases that appear to be typical; human judgments of typicality, even when made by purported experts, are notoriously unreliable and systematically biased. But judgmental samples do tend to be superior to either expediency or cluster samples, because the researcher can strive to approximate what he knows of the population's shape. This method is frequently employed in pilot studies and in participant observation.

Somewhat more objective is the quota sampling method, in which, say, men and women, whites and blacks, are selected in proportion to their numbers in the population. Although such procedures may minimize bias and unrepresentativeness in specific respects, the determination of which men and women, which whites and blacks, tends to be left to the convenience and haphazard judgment of the researcher, letting in through the back door all his or her selective biases.

More objective still is the systematic sampling method, in which a decision is made to select from the frame, in order, every fourth (or tenth, or twentieth) case. Such an advance decision removes the effects of tacit researcher preferences; if the ordering of cases within the frame is not stacked in some way, systematic sampling procedures usually yield approximately unbiased and representative samples.

Best of all, however, are probability sampling methods, which assure that every case in the sampling frame has a specified probability of being selected. At the root of probability methods is random sampling, which is not at all like haphazard or willy-nilly sampling. Random is a precise mathematical concept, meaning that any happening is strictly a matter of chance, through the operation of the mathematical laws of probability, like the flipping of a perfect coin or the rolling of perfect dice. In random sampling, the selection of cases is removed from the hands of the too-human researcher and turned over to some such random process. This ensures that each case has exactly the same probability of being selected, no matter which other cases may also be selected. Random sampling is thus completely unbiased, *as a method.* However, by chance alone, the sample resulting from this method could in rare instances still be biased. This possibility is precisely that of getting all heads in flipping a coin; such an outcome would not be unlikely through three flips but would be almost unimaginable through twenty flips of an honest coin. Thus, if a random sample is reasonably large, you can be practically certain that it is unbiased.

Because adequate random samples are unbiased, they tend also to be highly representative, though rarely perfectly so. If each person in the voter population has an equal chance of being selected, it follows that all categories of voters will be more or less proportionately represented in the sample. Therefore, the sample would roughly mirror the age shape of the entire population of voters.

But the real advantage of random sampling methods over all others is that because they are based on mathematical laws of probability, they also permit one to estimate the degree of sampling error—how more or less off the sample may be from the shape of the entire population. If we decide in advance how much sampling error we are willing to tolerate, these same laws of probability allow us to calculate precisely the sample size needed to come that close to the population-based answer.

Other probability sampling methods—more complex than simple random sampling—are even more powerful and more commonly employed in social research, but these methods are best left to more advanced texts.

POTENTIALS FOR FAILURE

Although the sampling plans of professional researchers are a great advance over the rather casual and often unconscious sampling procedures of the man in the street, they do not always guarantee success. Sampling error can at best be managed and kept within reasonable limits, never eliminated. Many careful investigations in all scientific fields have been completely undone by sampling error, but perhaps none of these disasters have received as much publicity as those in presidential election forecasting, such as the 1936 *Literary Digest* poll that predicted a landslide victory for Alf Landon over Franklin D. Roosevelt or the 1948 Gallup Poll that predicted Thomas Dewey would defeat Harry Truman.

Sampling plans are not always soundly formulated in every respect. The universe of cases may not be conceptualized with sufficient precision or, more commonly, the population of existing cases may be underidentified, omitting significant subpopulations of hidden cases. Prior information about the shape of that population may be seriously incomplete or incorrect. However, as our collective knowledge in a particular area increases, such inadequacies continue to diminish.

The most common failure of all, in professional research, is a mismatch between the sampling frame and the population it is supposed to represent. If significant segments of the population are omitted from the sampling frame, these cases have no chance whatsoever of turning up in the sample—making the sample biased or unrepresentative, or both. An example of this failure is the *Literary Digest* disaster, which used telephone directories and automobile registration lists as a sampling frame to represent American voters. Although such a sampling frame had proved adequate in preceeding elections, in 1936 much larger numbers of poor citizens, who did not own telephones or cars, turned out to vote, so that the frame poorly represented the actual population of active voters. Convenient sampling frames are generally risky, even when their correspondence to the population of interest seems much more direct than using automobile registration lists to identify voters. Student directories do not include all the students at a university, and existing voter registration lists do not include all those citizens who will vote in the next election. Although such lists can form the core of a sampling frame, they usually must be supplemented by other means to make them more inclusive, accurate, and up to date.

And, of course, even a sound sampling frame may be misused, consciously or otherwise, through unsound choice of sampling methods for selecting cases from the frame. In the 1948 Gallup Poll disaster, the failure was not so much one of sampling frame but rather the use of quota sampling methods. Even though today every professional researcher is fully aware of the superiority of probability sampling methods, these are not always employed nor are they always soundly applied. The researcher biases described in Chapter 2 are subtle and invidious and often creep through even the smallest cracks and joints within objective procedures.

But apart from the soundness with which a sampling plan is formulated, it is only a plan, and we all know that the best-laid plans of mice and men go oft awry. Employing carefully all the best sampling technology, we may select from a good sampling frame an unbiased and highly representative sample of cases, only to find that we cannot obtain the data we need about all the selected cases. In an interview study, for example, some of the persons selected have died, moved away, or are never at home; some others refuse to be interviewed or decline to answer particular questions. The sample we collect data on tends to be only a selective subset of the sample we had so carefully chosen, and through this slippage bias and unrepresentativeness creep back into the sampling process. Certain steps can be taken to diagnose and minimize these possibilities, but any slippage between the sample chosen and the sample obtained always increases the estimated sampling error.

There are three basic means of increasing the likelihood of a good sample that fits the shape of the larger universe of cases under study. First is scrutiny of prior information in that area, so we know more about the shape of the population. Second are pilot studies that explore the area and increase our knowledge, so that we aren't so much sampling in the dark. And third is replication by the research community at large, which has a good chance of picking up biases and unrepresentativeness. Each of these helps in getting a truer picture of the area we are investigating.

IMPORTANCE OF TIME

Sampling applies to much more than the finding or choosing of actual cases of whatever it is we wish to study. Equally important, for example, is the problem of selecting *times* at which we will study these cases. Any comparison of the various regions within the United States would produce very different results for the year 1800 than for the year 1900; last month's public opinion of presidential performance may be quite different from next month's.

Often, we want to study change itself, which requires examination of the same (or comparable) cases at more than one time. How many such time slices do we need to examine? And which time slices? For which cases? These decisions are vital aspects of the design of any inquiry, as we shall see more clearly in the chapters of Part III.

As in sampling more generally, the selection of appropriate time slices may run afoul of human blinders, blunders, and resource limitations. To minimize the impact of these potential problems requires the conscious formulation of an explicit sampling plan, following and adapting each of the steps described earlier. Even carefully deliberated plans for the selection of time slices can sometimes fail the investigator, for all the same reasons discussed in the preceeding section, but are surely better than implicit or even unconscious selections.

Sampling is a far more extensive and important matter than is ordinarily realized, because sampling (in the broadest sense) enters into every element of the research process. Before beginning an investigation, the researcher embodies only a sample of all the possible viewpoints and approaches. Only a sample of all pertinent questions are posed. Only a sample of all the cases in the subject area is examined, and for each case only a sampling of the data potentially available is obtained. Thus, one never gets all the data in either sense. One does only a sample of all possible analyses. Not all possible interpretations of results are looked at, and only a sample of all that was found is broadly communicated to others. Errors and biases are, of course, possible all along this line.

The inevitably limited and selective character of any single study is not grounds for becoming depressed, for it means only that no single study can ever find out the whole truth about an area. With careful coordination of all these broad sampling matters, a fairly small series of studies can give us a very accurate picture. Sampling is thus a positive and quite wondrous technology, without which meaningful research could never take place.

CHAPTER

6

DATA

Data are the raw materials for any and every inquiry. So how and where do we get them?

Data gathering can range from the simplicity of glancing outside the window to see if it is raining to an undertaking such as the United States census, so vast that banks of computers are required to keep track of the data. But simple or complex, there can be no research without data gathering, because this is the element that connects the inquiry with the empirical world. One can speculate or philosophize or create art or form convictions without data, but one cannot do research without data.

So what are data, these raw materials we need in order to work up answers to our research questions? Suppose you were on the road and were quite hungry. Daydreaming about food wouldn't help. You could use your eyes to look for cafe signs. You could stop and ask a gas station attendant about a good place to eat nearby. You could consult one of the published guides to restaurants in the area you're passing through. Such familiar procedures are fundamentally what a professional researcher uses in obtaining the data he or she needs. In other words, you've been gathering data all your life.

To get more of a grip on what data are, we must first distinguish them from information. The modern world is virtually awash with information—first-hand, second-hand, tenth-hand; accurate, distorted, or manipulated; useful, irrelevant, or meaningless. Information is simply input from the environment. Not all information is data for a specific investigation. When you were looking for a place to eat, if the gas station attendant had told you that it had rained earlier, that would be information but would not be data for your quest for food. Data are items of factual information that can be used in getting direct answers to research questions. From this simple definition, we can ferret out the criteria that distinguish data from other kinds of information.

First, data are items of empirically factual information. This one is more tricky than it first appears, because of the frequent blurring of fact and opinion. "There's a good place to eat at the end of this block" is an opinion that may or may not prove factual. Listeners continually confuse opinion and fact in the pronouncements of authorities and politicians. To say that John is surly may be only an opinion or a summary generalization, but we can record the fact that he snarled and walked off when greeted by his brother and believe that we have some real empirical data. If Jenny says that John is surly, we have only the fact that Jenny says John is surly.

A second criterion is that data must be *accurate* enough for our research questions. Information can be factual but still disqualify as data because it is inaccurate. We may factually see a cafe sign, only to pull up and discover the place is out of business, or that the place serves only Mexican food, which doesn't agree with our stomachs. The government may factually inform us that the Consumer Price Index is down, but is this accurate in terms of the local purchasing experience of the average citizen?

Factual information may not pass the accuracy test because it is too vague and general, or it is misleading and inadequate. If a fortune teller says you will meet someone in the future, this is no doubt factual, yet so generalized that it has little value. Information is most often misleading or inadequate when it is grossly incomplete. To the question "Where's Millie?", the answer "not here" gives us little help on our trail of truth. "They were together and John was yelling" can be very misleading if the report leaves off the phrase "because he stubbed his toe." We have all been misled a thousand times by such woefully incomplete information. Presenting only some of the facts is a fine art that all of us sometimes practice, but it will bedevil an investigation.

Inaccurate data can be worse than useless, because they will knock the remaining elements of the research process off the rails. Because data are the raw materials, faulty data will result in a faulty construction of answers and conclusions. In social research it is sometimes difficult to get accurate data because the actual scenes are covered by a screen of public relations and propaganda. There is a "PR front"—compounded of wariness and sociability—presented by virtually every organization, family, and person. How often does a policeman get a factual and fully accurate story from a speeding motorist? It is the official version of information that is routinely given out. Often, those who give it out are not being coy or secretive but themselves believe the official version, because organizations and persons alike tend to have limited knowledge and awareness of their own internal workings. People are so immersed in their own situations that they nearly always lack some distance, self-awareness, and objectivity about their own doings and internal processes. It is the researcher, then, who must supply these attributes in data gathering. This must be part of the investigator's craft.

Relevance is a third criterion. If we consult a travel guidebook, descriptions of festivals and annual pageants held in the area are information, but not relevant data in our search to be fed. (If we were instead seeking the location of a particular pageant, such descriptions might be data but the restaurant listings would be irrelevant information.) Data must be factual items we can *use* in the process of answering our research questions. This criterion has to do with the relative worth or value of information items for our current inquiry.

This one is also a bit tricky and requires some seasoned judgments by the inquirer, because seemingly irrelevant information can sometimes turn out to be vital data. In the hungry motorist example, if the station attendant remarks that he doesn't feel well, this offhand comment could point to the vital data that he suffered food poisoning at the cafe he was recommending. All research generates a certain amount of side information, some of which will sometimes turn out to contain vital clues to the problem at hand or related problems in that field. And, of course, what is side information for one investigation may be vital data for another.

The fourth and final criterion applies not to a single item but to the whole of a set of data. *Adequacy* of a set of data is a matter of its size and shape. Do we have enough data, and the right kinds of data, to get answers after we analyze and evaluate them? Getting adequate data involves simply persisting until one has them. The ordinary person is particularly prone to plunging ahead on the basis of inadequate data—with resulting stomach cramps, bad investments, needless surgery, and so on. Professional researchers are not immune to this mistake, but the guidelines of the research game reduce its incidence. If nothing else, professional colleagues are notorious for demanding an adequate data base to support the conclusions drawn.

To sum up these points, data are items of information that meet the four criteria of factualness, accuracy, relevance, and adequacy for a particular inquiry.

DATA RETENTION AND RETRIEVAL

Now that we have more of an idea of what data are, the question becomes what do we do with them? Like most raw materials, data must be treated and stored; it is not enough merely to obtain an adequate set of data. To be useful in research, the data must be somehow *retained* so they can be assembled and mobilized in some systematic fashion. In daily life, on the other hand, we tend to forget or overlook much of the pertinent information that has come our way and are thus often unable to call upon it when needed.

Here, too, we can see professional research as a refinement of ordinary inquiry. Professional investigators do not haphazardly gather data but systematically *collect* them. This crucial difference can perhaps be grasped if we liken data to coins. All of us continually acquire coins and let coins go in a fairly steady turnover. We usually have a certain store of coins on hand at any one time—a few in our pocket, a few on the dresser top, others here and there—but they all seem to come and go. We are something of a passive recipient of whatever coins are handed us, and we may or may not accumulate change for awhile, for one short-term purpose or another. A coin collector, on the other hand, actively seeks certain types of coins, in certain condition, to complete sets or to represent types of mint issues. Further, he or she usually systematically preserves, stores, and organizes the coins that have been obtained.

Ordinary inquiry often involves a rather casual and unplanned piling up of possibly useful information. Research involves a carefully planned, active search for specific kinds of information that will be kept in an organized manner, because retention and retrieval of data are as vital as their procurement.

COMPONENTS OF DATA COLLECTION

The real advantage that the professional investigator enjoys over the ordinary inquirer is an awareness of the need for objective, systematic, empirical *plans* for obtaining and storing data. Such plans of data collection involve four closely intertwined aspects: how to (1) evoke, (2) select, (3) encode, and (4) record data.

Data do not simply turn up in our pocket one day, any more than an 1861 Indian Head penny would. Usually data must be *evoked*, or actively elicited. That is, we must somehow actively arrange things so we are in a position to receive the data. Shoppers will discover which local papers carry grocery coupons, police may stake out a building, coffee buyers will open a bag of beans and stir them around, and social research observers will position themselves, both physically and socially, so they can find out what's going on.

Of course, not all the information evoked in such ways is data for our inquiry. We have to screen the signals from the noise, without tuning out anything vital. So we need some plan to *select* which information we will pay attention to.

The profound accomplishment of human intelligence is the ability to organize and make some sense out of the multitude of bits of information that impinge upon the human organism every moment of its existence. The key to this ability is our use of concepts and symbols. In daily living we use concepts to efficiently organize a mass of detailed information that would swamp NASA's finest computers. This is *encoding* at work. Because you are familiar with the concept of a van, you can summarize countless details of the machine parked out on the street simply by encoding it as "a blue Ford van," whereas a primitive jungle dweller would need to notice and keep track of hundreds of unfamiliar facts about it and would still have difficulty communicating that reality to others. To encode information is to summarize its bits under some mental concept and to thereafter refer to it by the symbol (code) which designates that concept. Thus, a certain activation of large numbers of receptors in the eye is encoded as "blue." This is why it is so important to thoroughly understand the basic concepts in any area we become interested in. These concepts allow us to represent to ourselves what it is that is out there—blue van, black hole, immunological system, consumer price index, and so on. Without these concepts, we are in that area in the position of our primitive jungle dweller. Encoding is entwined with the other aspects of data collection, because the concepts we use steer our evoking and selecting of information, to some extent, and are the means through which we usually record and organize data. New concepts (new ways of encoding environmental perceptions) often herald major break-throughs in science and application.

A final aspect of data collection—*recording*—may seem trivial, but it is really one of the things that separates the pro from the amateur in the business of finding out. Most people just settle for general impressions of grocery prices at different stores, of the growth performance of different kinds of stocks, and so on. For daily living, such general impressions are often quite good enough, but the research craft demands a careful, systematic recording of data.

The most efficient plan for recording data is to fully encode it first, and then enter the coded concept symbols into some kind of recording system. These code symbols of our concept can be words, letters, numbers, or anything else that is agreed upon and understood by all those involved. Such symbols are entered into the recording system by writing them down, circling one, punching holes into computer cards, and so on. The modern computer has greatly enhanced the ability to record and store vast amounts of data, and also to easily retrieve and analyze them.

The alternative type of plan is to record only partially encoded data—for example, taking written notes or shooting film footage—and to further encode these data later under more leisurely circumstances. In either case, the final form of recorded data will conform to the concepts and symbols of the encoding plan. The interrelationships among the various elements of research are demonstrated by the fact that the questions posed will almost certainly employ these very same concepts.

How do conscious, worked-out plans for evoking, selecting, encoding, and recording data improve the quality of an inquiry? In many different ways. Any sound plan for selecting data will enhance the relevance of those data, because fewer useless items of information will find their way into the study. Data adequacy is obviously increased by a plan for evoking data that involves a good sampling of the environment. Factualness and accuracy are markedly improved by careful recording, rather than a reliance on haphazard memory and general impressions.

An objective plan for all four aspects of data collection (evoking, selecting, encoding, and recording data) can sharply enhance all four criteria of data quality (factualness, accuracy, relevance, and adequacy). Objective data-collection plans differ from subjective ones in that they are deliberately worked out rather than impulsive, and they can be communicated to and followed successfully by other researchers with similar training and skills. We can tell you how the data were gathered for the latest national opinion survey or the testing of a new drug far more easily than we can tell you how El Greco got the data for his paintings.

Of course, the concepts we use for encoding and recording data can mislead as well as assist us. If they have built-in biases, the entire inquiry goes astray. For example, many IQ tests have come under heavy attack for measuring, not intelligence, but successful socialization into white, middle-class American mainstream society. But here too, the professional researcher is at least aware of these dangers and strives for increasingly unbiased and effective conceptions. Scientific or practical development in any field goes hand in hand with refinement of the concepts used to encode and record and communicate about the data in that field.

OBSERVATION METHODS

You can see these principles at work by looking at the major methods of data collection in social research.

Let us begin with observational methods. During school, most of us notice a fair amount of what takes place in the classrooms we attend, and some of what we notice we will remember for awhile. But the information we have available at the end of the semester is rarely a good enough data base for answering research questions about classroom interaction. Casual, offhand processes of noticing and remembering are no match for planned processes of watching and recording—that is, *observation*. The accuracy, relevance, factualness, and adequacy of the data resulting from a semester of systematic observation would certainly be superior.

We might still have some data gathering problems. For example, the observer may see the behavior but miss the action. That is, the concepts he uses to encode what he is observing may not reflect or capture what is really going on in the classroom. The observer might correctly note that laughter is occurring, but fail to distinguish "laugh-ing with" from "laughing at" the instructor. In social research, the concepts used in encoding must be both theoretically effective and empirically accurate in terms of the culture and shared understand-ings of those being observed. Otherwise, the observer is like the jungle dweller gazing at the van.

An additional problem is that the accuracy of what the observer sees may be thrown off by his very presence, as in the classroom example. Most people are not accustomed to strangers watching and recording their every move. In such circumstances people tend to act defensively, and off-the-record behaviors may be suppressed. An ob-server's plans for evoking data must always take account of these possibilities. Thus, a plan for evoking observational data might include postponing serious collection until the observer's presence has be-come accepted and taken for granted. For instance, as the class be-comes more accustomed to him and less apprehensive, reactions to his presence diminish rather quickly. Or the observer's presence might be concealed, by his pretending to be just another student or by indirect observation through one-way mirrors and concealed tele-vision cameras.

There also may be ethical issues. Will the data gathered be used against the students in any way? Does concealed observation involve moral or legal infringements? Any such ethical problems must be fully handled for the sake of all parties concerned.

In observational research, the process of evoking data—that is, bringing it about so the inquirer is in a position to receive data—is largely a matter of obtaining access to relevant situations. What one cannot find, or is not permitted to see, cannot be observed. So one often has to both seek appropriate situations and negotiate access to them, once found. Appropriate access also involves sampling, so that the situations observed are representative of the population of situa-tions being investigated. For instance, in the classroom example, merely observing the first day of class and the final exam period would obviously be an unrepresentative sample of classroom inter-action.

The access one gains to situations must also be such that one is in a position to receive the data needed. If a classroom investigator can sit only in the back of the room, for instance, his view and per-spective are greatly restricted, so arrangements to sit in different locations during different periods would be better. An investigator must often be clever in utilizing the partial access he gains for all it is worth in data collection, because partial and conditional access is the usual case. But if the investigator is decent about it and displays no shoddy purpose, it is surprising how many situations one can gain access to.

INTERVIEW METHODS

Let's next look at *interview methods*, which are the ones most frequently employed in social research because they are cheaper and more flexible than observation. In a single interview, data can be collected about the past and the future as well as the present moment, about innermost feelings as well as displayed behavior, and about secret doings as well as public displays.

But these advantages of interviewing may be bought at some price in both the factualness and the accuracy of the data. This is so because we are relying on what people say the information is, rather than on our direct perceptions. There are often reliability cross-checks, such as interviewing other witnesses and participants, but one is still operating on hearsay evidence about the situations under study. On a sensitive issue, for instance, voters may tell a pollster one thing and act quite differently in the anonymous privacy of the voting booth. Interview methods face each of the problems in evoking data that observation does plus a few distinctive ones of its own. For example, access is a concern in interviewing too; can we get the right people to talk with us about the things we want to know? Some respondents may refuse to be interviewed, and others may decline to answer certain important questions. More important and more often, many of those who do cooperate cannot accurately give us the information we need. Try it yourself. What was the name of your kindergarten teacher? What did you do the weekend before last Christmas? Who was the defeated vice-presidential candidate in the last election? (We didn't do too well on these either.) The difficulty of answering such questions as these does not deter most people from giving an interviewer their best guesses as though they were solid data. But you can see how factualness and accuracy may be a bit at risk.

Even though we are all accustomed to answering questions, an interview is usually an unfamiliar situation that may provoke some apprehension. Here is a perfect stranger, persistently pursuing a line of questioning about matters we may not be used to discussing, and he is recording our every answer. Why does he want to know these things? What does he think of me and my answers? What is he going to do with this information? People tend to react warily in interview situations, choosing what they say "for the record." So, just as in observation, some data may be suppressed or distorted.

What sets interview methods apart from observation is the more active strategy of evoking data, by asking questions to elicit the statements we record. Asking questions is a fine art; if you ask a silly question, you get silly answers. There is often a mismatch between the concepts and symbols of the asker and those of the answerer. Thus the asker may not accurately communicate his questions to the answerer, and the answerer may be unable to accurately communicate his responses to the asker. Such misunderstandings, caused by differences in language and backgrounds, are a major source of inaccuracy in interview data. For instance, the question "What are your reference groups?" doesn't communicate well to the majority of the populace because they haven't taken sociology courses. Similarly, the response "She's my main squeeze" may be improperly understood, encoded, and recorded by a middle-class interviewer who hasn't been around. Askers tend to routinely overestimate the awareness of respondents toward the concepts and perspectives of the inquirer, and respondents overestimate the savvy of the askers about their particular speech patterns and background.

Plans for collecting data through interviews—and their paper cousin, the questionnaire—must take these potential difficulties into account and build in safeguards to minimize their effects. The questions are carefully formulated and perhaps pilot-tested to see that they reflect the basic research questions and effectively communicate to the answerers. This also helps to avoid those loaded, ambiguous, or double-barreled questions so common in ordinary social conversation. The other main approach is training and preparing the askers to minimize reactions through dress, manner of approach, development of rapport, and so on.

These work. And for all their pitfalls, interview methods have proved to be a very efficient and cost-effective way to get a lot of good data. No policeman, teacher, social worker, or social researcher operates without using them rather routinely.

SECONDARY RESEARCH

The third major means for obtaining data in social research or in life is to borrow them from others rather than collect them oneself. This can be the most cost-effective of all, because the data are usually packaged already (evoked, selected, encoded, and recorded). This method is called *secondary research* or secondary analysis because we do a second round of data collection from among those data others have already gathered. The efficiency of this method can be fantastic. For instance, compare checking census tables to find out how many people live in a city with doing your own headcount from scratch. Blessed is the inquirer who finds out others have done a great deal of his legwork for him.

But to borrow data is not to escape any of the problems of data quality and accuracy; it is only to borrow the problems of the original collector. How the problems and the promise of borrowed data are managed is the subject of Chapter 11. For now, it is enough to say that the problems are essentially the same, but plans for coping with them are necessarily a bit distinctive.

EXPERIMENTAL METHODS

Experiments are the fourth and final major means of data collection. Experimental methods, too, involve painstaking planning and incorporate numerous safeguards for quality of data, but it can be a real trick to simulate real life conditions and events in the laboratory. (The technology of field experiments has arisen to cope with these lab simulation problems.) Also, in social research and the policy sciences, experiments are often barred because of ethics. We can split molecules and note the results, but it is not ethical to split families to see what happens. Yet, the experimental method is far more flexible than is sometimes realized, as we will see in Chapter 14.

INTEGRITY IN DATA COLLECTION

This leads us to a more general point about *integrity* in data collection. After all, social researchers are in the business because they have a profound interest in people and all their doings. Just as the reputable coin collector does not deface coins and reputable physicians will not do capricious harm to their patients, so reputable social researchers will not deface or do serious harm to the very thing they are driven to study. Data collection always carries with it the possibility of doing harm to others, and these risks must always be minimized. For example, many a newsman has created unwanted notoriety for those investigated and reported on, sometimes resulting in unjust losses for the people involved. Any potential harms must always be weighed against the likely benefits, if any, to those who are studied, just as in the honest practice of medicine.

Integrity enters into all aspects of data collection. Data evoked through deception or misrepresentation can produce serious social and even legal consequences for the investigators. There are also risks that anonymity or confidentiality will be abused, or that records will be stolen or subpoenaed and put to less honorable uses. Integrity is essential in the more general sense of not fudging or misrepresenting the data or burying those data that do not fit one's schemes. To pursue an inquiry in the professional manner is not only to employ highly technical skills but, equally, to embrace professional responsibilities to society and the wheel of collective human intelligence.

Data are the input we receive back from our interactions with the environment. Any data, if true, are probably better than no data, because they are our connection with the real world. For the layman, data input provides a continuous feedback with which one can correct one's course and achieve one's plans of action. For both laymen and professionals, data are the traffic across our research bridge from reality to our conceptual models.

But our work of finding out is not done. Data are the raw materials, but we must yet extract answers from them through measurement, analysis, and evaluation.

CHAPTER

7

MEASUREMENT

Raw data are the raw materials from which findings are eventually fashioned. After the data are gathered and encoded, they must be further packaged before being analyzed and evaluated. This packaging involves two tasks which are usually carried on simultaneously: classifying the encoded data, and digesting or summarizing the set of data into some more manageable form. Both of these are essentially matters of *measurement.*

Human beings always do this packaging of data, whether consciously or not, as the means of reducing a multitude of bits of perceptual information into summary forms with which they can reason and evaluate. Consider the alternative, for instance, of aimlessly rummaging through 10,000 questionnaires. Those who do poorly at this step of packaging become buried in details and have trouble getting to any bottom lines.

In life situations, we have learned to categorize and digest data as part of growing up in our particular culture and historical time. In research, this step is usually carefully planned as the research is being designed.

Measurement may seem like a humdrum subject, but let's look again. Along the trail from quest to conclusion we always get involved in some measuring and gauging. In fact, measurement is an ever-present aspect of all human perception. That is, we go around measuring things all the time. No child could survive into adulthood without developing considerable practical skill at measurement, and in daily life we constantly measure and are measured by others. So we are no strangers to the subject.

We count calories, step on the bathroom scales, and estimate whether a letter needs two postage stamps or only one. Others are always assessing our age, height, weight, body temperature, emotional mood, credit rating, IQ, classroom performance, or life expectancy. Measurement is so much second nature to us that we even measure just for the fun of it: singles rate the attractiveness of the opposite sex, in search of the perfect "10"; sports fans debate the exact length of a prodigious home run; and fishing enthusiasts talk excitedly about the size of the one that got away.

Measurement is so second nature to us that it draws our attention only under unusual conditions—when another driver misjudges distances and bashes in our fender or, conversely, when someone displays exceptional skill at it. We notice measurement, too, when we are struggling to master some new skill like typing or driving a nail or skateboarding. But as we master any activity, the measuring aspect drops into the background and becomes more second nature to us.

Measurement is the process of determining where a given case falls along some variable. You'll recall from Chapter 2 that a variable is any feature that can vary in type or degree from case to case. Consider, for example, the variable of physical attractiveness of persons; we can all agree that persons vary from one another in attractiveness, even though we probably won't agree on exactly what constitutes attractiveness.

Some of us may think mainly of differences in kind, or type, of attractiveness, distinguishing, perhaps, between "handsome" for males and "pretty" for females. Using a conceptual scheme of this sort to locate a given person along the variable of attractiveness is *nominal* measurement, naming the kind, type, or category this case represents. There's no more or less of something in a nominal variable; the categories are simply different from one another, for example, types of dogs or kinds of fruit.

But probably most often, when we speak of measurement, we are instead thinking of variation in degree rather than type—*how* attractive is the person, rather than what sort of attractiveness that person has. We want to know where this case falls along a dimension or continuum of attractiveness, ranging from the lowest possible degree to the highest possible degree.

Sometimes the best we can do toward this end is to agree that these people are "highly attractive," these are "fairly attractive," these are "rather plain," and these are "not at all attractive." Using a conceptual scheme of this sort amounts to *ordinal* measurement: judgments of more and less. The conceptual categories that are distinguished are definitely rank-ordered in degree; we would know, for example, that someone classified as "fairly attractive" is more attractive than some but less attractive than some others. However, we would not be able to say how much more or how much less.

To do so would require us to establish some standard unit of measurement, some uniform basic quantity of degree such as the inch, the pound, or the Fahrenheit degree of temperature. Then we could determine that, say, Ann is four units higher in attractiveness than Carol; that is, we could determine how many units it would take to span the interval of attractiveness that separates Ann and Carol. *Interval* measurement of this sort can be difficult to establish objectively, but we sometimes resort to rather subjective versions in the form of "rating scales," such as the infamous "1 to 10" scale of girl-watchers and boy-watchers. The fundamental problem here is that the unit of attractiveness is only subjectively defined, so that the same person is likely to receive widely different scores from any two raters, whereas true interval measurement with objective units of measurement leads to close agreement between measurers. Moreover, it is nearly impossible with rating scales to ensure that the difference between a "3" and a "5" is precisely the same as that between a "7" and a "9," whereas this would be no problem in the case of, say, a Fahrenheit thermometer where the units are objectively established.

The final refinement in measuring variation in degree is the establishment of a nonarbitrary zero point. We understand and agree what it is for something to have absolutely no length, no weight, or no heat, but we lack any such understanding and agreement about what it is for a person to have absolutely no physical attractiveness or no ability to play the piano. Therefore, it makes no more sense to say that Ann is twice as attractive as Carol than it does to say that 20 degrees Fahrenheit is twice as warm as 10 degrees. (Think carefully about that one, remembering that zero on the Fahrenheit scale is a completely arbitrary point that was established by setting it equal to the coldest moment in one particular winter in one little Alpine village.) Measurement schemes that combine a standard unit of measurement, such as the inch, with an absolute zero point provide *ratio* measurement, allowing us to express variation in degree between two cases as a ratio of their scores: this cigar is 1.312 times as long as that one.

Each type of scale is distinctive and useful. In nominal scales we can classify or categorize, but we cannot rank the categories in any way. In ordinal scales we can categorize and also rank the categories. In interval scales we can categorize, rank the categories, and also determine how much more or less. In ratio scales we can do all of these as well as determine the ratio of one category to another—ten miles is twice as far as five miles.

We routinely employ all four of these levels of measurement in daily life, without giving much thought to it. The use of yardsticks, bathroom scales, and thermometers—well-established and objective procedures yielding true interval and even ratio measurements—has been taken for granted since childhood. But how often do we actually use them? More commonly we merely *estimate* even simple physical measures: "We must have been here for about two hours now"; "It must be 90 degrees outside"; and "That carpet looks to be about 8 by 14." When daily life measurement turns from the physical world to the realm of social and psychological features, we have little recourse. There are no handy objective and well-established procedures for measurement, against which we can, through experience, calibrate our rough-and-ready assessments of cheerfulness, attractiveness, or loyalty. The subjective nature of such assessments seldom allows us to achieve more than crude nominal and ordinal measures; we may sometimes employ crude rating scales or even speak loosely of someone being twice as nice as someone else, but we always realize that such approximations to interval or ratio measurements are shaky.

There is always some measurement in any finding out endeavor, even if it is only measurement of the "ballpark approximation" kind: "It's about twenty minutes to the airport," "He's very tall for an Oriental," or "She's more cheerful today." Sometimes such measurement is quite good enough, at least in everyday living. But in social research it usually is not; researchers must be less subjective and offhand, more accurate and more precise.

ROLE OF MEASUREMENT

In the research process, measurement serves as a bridge between the encoding aspect of data collection and the element of data analysis (which will be described in Chapter 8). Many of the most powerful methods of data analysis require measurements as inputs; raw data must first be transformed into measurements. Sometimes this transforming takes place after the data have already been encoded and recorded. An example is the grading of a school exam; your answer to each test item is encoded as, say, correct or incorrect, and then the number of correct answers is counted up. Later the instructor transforms this information into a grade: an ordinal measurement such as A, B, C, D, or F. When measurements are constructed from previously encoded and recorded data, the measurement process amounts to a preliminary stage in data analysis. On the other hand, some measurements are direct rather than constructed; for example, a questionnaire item may ask you to report your exact age in years. Your response to this single item serves as a direct (ratio level) measurement of your age, so that in such cases the process of measurement is handled in the very process of encoding. This should not be surprising, because both encoding and measurement involve fitting the gathered data into some pre-established system of concepts.

The essential difference between encoding and measurement has to do with their respective levels of conceptualization of information. To look at your exam paper and encode the answers as correct or incorrect involves some appreciable level of conceptual abstraction, but this is not the level upon which the eventual analysis will be conducted to answer the question of how satisfactorily you have performed in some course. To answer that question the instructor first needs to assign a letter grade to this exam and to each of your other course assignments. Measurement is the step that raises the conceptualization of information up to that level necessary to analyze the data. Measurement is thus a key step in the refinement of raw data into materials suitable for working out the answer to a research question.

Concepts not only allow us to represent information to ourselves but also tell us what to look for. The system of concepts that comprise a measure of a variable provides a set of indicators to look for in trying to determine where a given case falls along that variable. One pattern of indicators would suggest that the person is "pretty" whereas another pattern would indicate "handsome." Certain patterns of correct and incorrect test items would indicate a grade of A, and other patterns would suggest different grades. How well our concepts in a particular subject area organize the data and mirror the realities of that slice of the environment is a good indication of our state of knowledge. A science travels forward on its concepts.

The major difference between measurement in daily life and in research is the objectivity with which these patterns of indicators are spelled out and used in assessment. The professional researcher self-consciously formulates explicit plans for measurement that can be communicated to and followed by other investigators. For each conceptual category of location of cases along the variable, such a plan specifies a definite pattern of indicators and explicit procedures for matching these specified patterns against the facts of particular cases. For example, a medical researcher would categorize the results of some treatment in exact terms of blood pressure readings, temperature, levels of various substances in a blood sample, and so on, whereas a layman might simply note that his friend is feeling better.

These plans for measurement can become quite complex and technically demanding, especially when they strive to provide interval or ratio levels. Details of measurement procedures are better left to more advanced texts. What is important here is to recognize that the greater objectivity of scientific measurement does not in itself guarantee better measurement than the casual procedures of everyday intelligence.

CRITERIA OF MEASUREMENT

What do we really want in a measure? Commonly endorsed criteria of measurement include *accuracy, precision, reliability,* and *validity.* Each of these criteria is important, but they overlap considerably. Perhaps the best way to come to grips with these is to think about what you want from your bathroom scales at home.

First, you want an accurate reading of your weight; that is, what the scales say about your weight should be factually correct. Accuracy in this sense is easy to obtain, provided you are not too fussy about precision. Suppose the scales had only two possible readings: "under 100 pounds" and "at least 100 pounds." It should be easy enough to adjust the spring tension to make sure that almost everyone would be accurately classified in terms of these two categories. But each category takes in an awful lot of territory and thus fails to make distinctions among people who obviously differ markedly in weight. You would probably prefer your scales to make much more discriminating distinctions; that is, you would like greater precision of measurement—say, to the nearest pound. The problem is that readings expressed in specific pounds are bound to give a wrong answer in quite a few cases, no matter how we adjust the spring tension. In measurement of any kind there is a built-in trade-off between accuracy and precision; the more you demand of one, the less you get of the other. The best general rule for dealing with this dilemma is to go for no more precision than is absolutely necessary, to achieve the most accuracy (within this range of precision). A degree of precision that exceeds the bounds of reasonable accuracy is false precision.

Reliability is also a common problem with all measurements, including bathroom scales; they often fail to give consistent and dependable readings. If you weigh yourself again 10 seconds later, you would like the machine to give you almost exactly the same reading—stability of measurement. Moreover, you would like your scales to give readings that are consistent with those from other scales—for example, your doctor's scales. But we all have learned that such equivalence of measurement is rare. Readings that are unreliable (in either or both of these respects) make it difficult to determine your current weight with any degree of accuracy or even confidence. Social research interviewers, for instance, should reliably assess their respondents' answers, whatever the time of day and whatever their own mood. The same response scores should be elicited, whichever interviewer is doing the asking.

Finally, you would like bathroom scale readings to actually reflect your weight, and not also some other extraneous variable. Many bathroom scales give different readings depending on just which spot on the bathroom floor you place the touchy little machine; in that case, the reading it gives is only in part a measure of your weight and also in part a measure of where the scale is located. Similarly, some scales seem to be sensitive to the amount of load-bearing surface area, so that persons of identical weight—one with big feet and one with small—get different readings. To the extent that readings are influenced by extraneous variables in addition to (or, worse, instead of) the variable these readings are meant to reflect, the measurements suffer in validity. In the social sciences also, we take great pains to see that extraneous variables are not entering into our measurements to mask or distort our readings.

Good measures, then, are those that have accuracy, precision, reliability, and validity sufficient for our current purposes. If our purpose is merely to make sure we have not gained a lot of weight, we need not make stringent demands on the qualities of measurement. But if we are trying to qualify for a certain weight-class in a wrestling tournament, or trying to determine body size in calculating what dosage of a powerful drug the patient's body can withstand, we need very good measurement.

These four criteria apply in any subject area. In less developed areas such as the social sciences, we must, if anything, be even more alert to them because of the crude and subjective nature of our measurements at this time.

MEASUREMENT ERROR

In research and in life we are most concerned with getting things into the right categories on one of our scales. *Measurement error* is the misclassifying of a case. That is, we have failed to correctly determine where something falls along some conceptual variable and we suffer the consequences of that failure. In real life this can involve crumpled fenders, the shelling of one's own troops, prescribing the wrong medicine, and so on. In research, measurement errors can impede our progress from quest to correct and valuable conclusions. It is interesting that what we ordinarily call good judgment in people is actually good measurement, a knack for correctly categorizing.

Such error is thus mainly a matter of inaccuracy of measurement. How seriously such errors affect a given inquiry depends on how many we make, how far off these misclassifications are, and whether there is any pattern to these misclassifications.

The consequences of frequency and size of errors are too obvious to belabor; a great number of even small errors, or just a few rather large errors are enough to throw us off the trail of truth. But the matter of patterns of error may be a less familiar concern. For example, there may be some pattern to the *direction* of errors—a fairly consistent pattern of over-estimation or underestimation. The readings from the bathroom scales might be systematically inaccurate; perhaps every reading is always two pounds too high (or too low). Constant errors of this sort are not too serious, for they do not affect the accuracy of any comparisons we might make between people, and by subtracting two pounds we can accurately gauge the absolute weight of each person. More troublesome are the less systematic patterns of direction of errors, as when the bathroom scales sometimes read too heavy and sometimes too light. Such unreliability of measurement distorts comparisons between people; some who actually weigh the same will appear to differ, and some who actually differ in weight will seem to weigh the same. Moreover, there is no uniform adjustment we can make to retrieve individuals' absolute weights. Such errors operate in the same way that static and noise interfere with good radio reception; they obscure the clarity of our results. Only if the number of overestimates is more or less equal to the number of underestimates—as though the direction of errors were random—do we have technical means of partly compensating for nonsystematic errors.

A quite different sort of patterning of errors has to do with how measurement errors relate to the true scores of the various cases. That is, the direction or size of error may be related to the true score of a given case. For example, most bathroom scales are more accurate in certain weight ranges than others. Many manufacturers warn that the machine does not give very accurate readings for weights under twenty pounds. It is not uncommon for scales to underestimate the weight of very light persons and to overestimate that of very heavy persons, but to perform well in the middle ranges. Thus, the direction and size of error depends on one's true weight. Such correlated error seriously affects the accuracy and validity of measurement because it systematically biases comparisons among persons—in this case, exaggerating differences between persons at the two extremes of weight. Various patterns of measurement error are illustrated in Figure 6.

Measurement error is a significant concern in social research, as it is in other endeavors. The sources of measurement error are legion. Consider again the example of grades on an examination, which are meant to measure only knowledge of the subject matter of the course; any other influences on the grades must be considered to be sources of measurement error. Two students who have the same degree of knowledge and competence may yet receive different grades through the error-generating influences of a great many factors. One student may have less skill in reading comprehension, so that he works more slowly or misreads certain test items. Perhaps one student is bored, ill, sleepy, or upset during the exam, causing his performance to suffer. Or one student may be seated near the door and is constantly distracted by the noises in the hallway. Perhaps the mimeographing of the exam was imperfect, so that a key

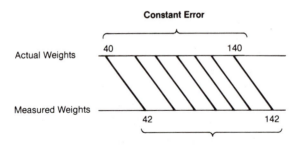

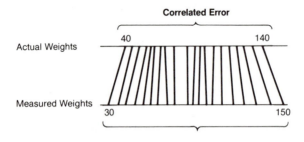

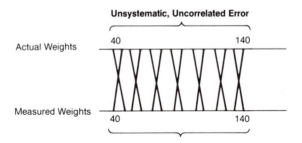

FIGURE 6. Effects of Various Patterns of Measurement Error

word was smudged or missing on one student's copy. Neither student was able to review all the course materials in preparing for the exam, but one was wiser or luckier in that the chapter he didn't get to did not provide any items for this exam. Test items are often ambiguous in what they ask for; one student's interpretation of these ambiguities may chance to be more appropriate, matching the slant of the instructor, or perhaps one asks the instructor for clarification while the other does not. Or one of the students may accidentally place his check mark in the wrong box, even though he knew the right answer. In grading the exams, the instructor may make mistakes in encoding the answers as correct or incorrect, or may miscount the number of correct answers. Even instructor bias in the eventual assignment of letter grades has to be considered.

You will recognize that many of these sources of measurement error actually arise in the process of data collection itself. Poor quality data always result in substantial error of measurement. The most important step in preventing or minimizing measurement error is the careful execution of well-formulated plans for evoking, selecting, encoding, and recording data to ensure their factuality, accuracy, relevance, and adequacy. Measurement is an element where the professional—researcher or practitioner—really shines. In practical fields, the correct diagnosing of situations and the ability to spot and correct gross errors show that the worker has mastered the craft of measurement in his field. In research, our own times have witnessed a host of technological breakthroughs that have opened the door to inquiries once impossible before these developments. But the fundamentals of measurement remain the same.

In the real world, some measurement error is virtually inevitable. The inquirer may introduce it simply by being there, as we have seen in earlier chapters. But we don't strive for perfect measurement, only for measurement that is good enough for our research purposes. If we pay sufficient heed to accuracy, precision, reliability, and validity, we can do this successfully.

CHAPTER

8

ANALYSIS

Now that we have gathered some data, we need to *analyze* them to see what they say. Analysis is what you do with data. After all the encodings and measurements, what do the data show? What answers do the data suggest? What evidence do the data provide? Without analysis, we would simply be left with piles of unrelated and undigested information.

In everyday life most data analysis is swift, informal, and only semi-conscious. The experienced freeway driver glances at the multitude of bits of perceptual data and comes up with the pattern "accident in the left lane somewhere over that hill." Or the experienced police officer notices a hundred small details and senses an ambush. In professional social research, however, data analysis tends to be methodical, highly formalized, and very explicit. A closetful of standardized questionnaires is laboriously translated into a few boxes of computer cards, which yield stacks of statistical printout showing that, for instance, 82.4 percent of homeowners also own at least one automobile.

But the essentials of the process are the same. Data analysis is first a matter of *finding the patterns* (if any) among the digested data on hand. The data are reviewed and examined in hopes of recognizing some definite shape to the set of facts—some trends, directions, configurations, proportions, relationships, or the like.

Patterns, then, are specific forms of interconnections among facts. There can, of course, be many different kinds of patterns. Sometimes we are interested in logical interconnections: a social worker notes, for instance, that child abuse in the Smelser family occurs only when the husband is present and never when he is away. Or the interconnections may be conceptual in nature: everything considered, the platypus, even though it lays eggs, is actually a mammal. Spatial relations are another familiar source of patterning: we notice from detailed maps that Indianapolis is practically circular in form. Patterns that depend on interconnections of these (or similar) kinds are *qualitative* or non-numerical patterns. Recognizing qualitative patterns in a set of facts is an important and well-practiced aspect of ordinary human intelligence that figures prominently in social research as well. The finding of such qualitative patterns is the essence of much participant observation field research, of ethnographies, and case studies.

Much less commonly appreciated is the extent to which everyday thinking also seeks out quantitative patterns in data, that is, forms of numerical or statistical interconnections among facts. The most ordinary conversations are filled with expressions that reflect patterns of crude counts or crude measurements of degree. For example, we observe that "In their lifetimes, very few bowlers ever roll a perfect game" or that "Most grocery prices went up this month." No specific percentages are mentioned in such statements, so they are only crudely or quasi-statistical statements. Yet, you can plainly see that any statement that includes such ideas as "all, most, many, few, or none," "always, usually, never," "average or typical," and so on, implicitly refers to some underlying statistical frequency distribution. Moreover, many of the patterns found by ordinary inquiry implicitly refer to statistical relationships between measured variables: "The smaller strawberries tend to be tastier" or "When I exercise I usually feel better the rest of the day."

Qualitative analysis of data, in social research, is a careful examination of data in search of qualitative or quasi-statistical patterns of just these sorts. Thus, an anthropologist looks for the child rearing pattern in a native tribe, a sociologist looks for typical adjustment patterns among single parents, and a doctor looks for the patterns underlying a patient's symptoms and complaints. *Quantitative analysis* of data involves a formal search for patterns that are quantitative in the strict sense—explicitly numerical or truly statistical. Examples would be the pattern of percentage returns, adjusted for inflation, on various types of investments over the last ten years, or the pattern of recovery rates produced by some new treatment. To undertake quantitative analysis of data places greater demands on the adequacy with which they have been measured; statistical analysis requires data with reasonably precise and accurate measurement, whereas the cruder and approximate measures of everyday inquiry may be adequate for discerning qualitative and even quasi-statistical patterns.

ERRORS IN ANALYSIS

Analysis can obviously go astray, both in life and in professional research. In either qualitative or quantitative analysis, two types of fundamental errors can be made: false negatives and false positives. The false negative type involves finding no pattern when one actually exists. Such errors can stem from many sources: insufficient familiarity with the subject so that the existing pattern is missed, prior expectations and fixed ideas that blind the inquirer to an existing pattern, which differs from what was anticipated, and so on. The data may also be insufficient to display what is really out there. The main point here is that patterns do not step forward and make themselves known to the waiting investigator; rather, the investigator must seek and find them. This is one facet of the craft of finding something out.

Professional researchers have again and again, in every area, eventually found patterns, regularities, and natural laws amongst data where the ordinary populace has seen nothing. The promise of science is that by skillful and persistent application of the research rules to every element we can greatly increase our understanding, prediction, and control of any conceivable aspect of reality.

The false positive type of error involves concluding that a pattern exists among the data when in reality it does not. Sometimes this is a matter of seeing what one wants to see instead of what is actually there. Or it may stem from overoptimism about some slight and insignificant trends. It may involve falsely assuming a connection between variables when something entirely different actually caused the result: one might foolishly assert that air travel causes crime, because both air travel and crime rates have increased over the last few decades, or that drinking milk causes alcoholism, because virtually all alcoholics were found to have drunk milk as children. At worst, one's preconceptions, fixed ideas, and prejudices may lead one to assert patterns when there is absolutely no real evidence that they exist.

Scientific research has some safeguards against both false negatives and false positives. There is a strong tradition of replicating studies under the same conditions and different conditions to verify that the patterns are indeed real. The data from most studies in most fields are also made available to other inquirers, so that they may seek patterns that others failed to find. And in more quantitative studies, the probability of either error type can be computed and is routinely published along with the findings.

Avoiding the false negative type of mistake is partly a matter of perceiving and recognizing the patterns among data, and this rests upon experience, skill, and insight into the area. Avoiding the false positive type of mistake rests particularly on the honest willingness to see that an expected or hoped for pattern of data actually is not there. In part, the standardized analysis procedures of professional research exist to guard against these two types of errors, but these safeguards are only mechanical and must be applied by humans who are both more creative and more fallible.

INFERENCES, PROBABILITIES, AND STATISTICS

Patterns of data may be direct answers to a research question, or may only be clues useful to answering it. For example, if the question were "What kind of beast is the platypus?" then our recognizing the platypus to be a mammal would be a direct answer. If the question were "How many species of mammals are found in Australia?" that same pattern would only be a clue or a stepping-stone.

Because data analysis amounts to using data to reason our way to an answer, data analysis always involves the skills—though not always the rules—of logical *inference*. Students of human intelligence have been fond of documenting the surprising extent to which ordinary reasoning is plagued by various logical fallacies. We have seen examples of these in earlier chapters: overgeneralizing from an instance or two; backward reasoning, where one adopts a conviction and then looks for confirming evidence; circular reasoning, where, for instance, Republicans are right because they think like me, and they think like me because they are right; and so on. But even though everyday thinking often ignores and sometimes violates the rules of logic, the average human generally makes sound and defensible inferences from the facts at hand.

For instance, suppose you chanced to meet a fellow by the

name of Wiseheart. This is an interesting name, and it causes you to remember that your cousin in Milwaukee is a typist for an architectural firm: Adam Wiseheart Associates. As you continue chatting with the Wiseheart you've just met, further interesting facts emerge: his first name, too, is Adam, he is from Milwaukee, and he is an architect. Even a fairly young child would make the obvious inference that this fellow must be your cousin's employer.

Even if it turns out to be incorrect, one need not be ashamed. The inference is a reasonable, defensible, and justifiable piece of inductive reasoning. Because both the first and the last names are quite uncommon in our experience, it is not very likely that two different persons would have such a distinctive name. And there can't be many architects in even a large place like Milwaukee. It is very improbable that two different persons taken at random should have the same distinctive name, the same profession, and the same hometown; such a coincidence would be almost incredible. With a bit of work, statisticians could calculate the chances of such a coincidence, and they would find it to be one chance out of several million. So it is perfectly reasonable to suppose that this fellow is indeed your cousin's boss.

Inductive reasoning of this kind is the sort of logical inference most central to the analysis of data. Unlike deductive reasoning, inductive reasoning leads to likely or plausible conclusions rather than demonstrated conclusions. *Inductive reasoning* is a matter of evidence, whereas *deductive reasoning* is a matter of proof. Data rarely provide proof, only more or less strong evidence. *Probability*, rather than certainty, is the coin of data analysis. And where probability enters in, *statistics* cannot be far behind.

One of the key differences between everyday inquiry and professional research lies in their differing uses of the tools of probability and statistics in analyzing data.

Probability plays a large part in everyday thinking:

- "My sunglasses are probably still in the car."
- "I'm almost certain it won't rain today."
- "I'll give you 2-to-1 odds on the ballgame tonight."
- "Chances are, we'll meet again."

Probability is nothing more than a measure of likelihood. But as with most measurements in everyday life, ordinary measurements of probability are crude "ballpark estimates," or *subjective* probabilities. We have already seen that subjective probabilities, however crude, often permit highly effective inductive reasoning. But as with measurement more generally, the carefully constructed objective measurement procedures of professional researchers yield more precise and more accurate measures of likelihood: *objective* probabilities. The difference can be seen clearly in the playing of card games. The ordinary player uses subjective probabilities: "based on what I've seen, he probably doesn't have an ace in his hand, so I'll play these cards." Some professional gamblers, however, are proficient at rapid calculation of the precise objective probability that the other player holds an ace.

Statistics, too, are used differently in everyday thinking and in professional research. Everyday thinking tends to rely on quasi statistics: subjective estimates of relative frequency and of statistical relationship between crudely measured variables. Again, such quasi statistics are often quite good enough for everyday purposes but are less precise or accurate than calculated statistics. It may be enough for the casual shopper to know that "very few of these apples are bruised," but the produce manager for the supermarket needs to know just what percentage are bruised.

A second and more subtle difference concerns the type of statistical strategy used. The strategy of inductive reasoning followed in everyday thinking resembles that of Bayesian statistics. Suppose the idea somehow comes to you that most men carrying briefcases are also wearing neckties. You think that's probably true, and you search your memory for whatever data you have accumulated; perhaps for a day or so you pay particular attention to men you encounter who are carrying briefcases. If through these searches you see only a couple of exceptions to the rule, you are even more confident that it is true. The logic of this strategy of statistical analysis of data is a powerful one, although in everyday life it is employed only quasi-statistically, with poorly estimated subjective probabilities, nonprobability sampling of data, and an absence of any formal calculations.

Most researchers, on the other hand, follow a data analysis strategy of classical statistics—not responding to each case as it comes in, but waiting until all the data from a carefully designed sample of briefcase-toting men are in. Formal descriptive statistics (such as percentages, averages, and the like) are explicitly calculated from the sample data. These sample-based statistics are then used to calculate the objective probabilities that certain precise patterns hold true in the larger population of cases from which the sample was drawn. For instance, the sample data may show that 84.12 percent of men carrying briefcases are wearing ties; then, depending on the size and quality of the sample, a researcher may be able to infer (with 99 percent confidence) that the true percentage within the larger population is not less than 79.1 and not greater than 89.1.

This difference in statistical strategy follows rather straightforwardly from the reliance of everyday intelligence on casual accumulation of data and the reliance of professional research upon the systematic collection of data.

DATA PROCESSING

Finding patterns in data and using these patterns to reason our way to an answer is seldom an easy matter. Whether we have too many data or too few, it is often difficult to see the forest for the trees. An orderly and systematic arrangement of data makes it easier for us to recognize any patterns that exist in the data and less likely that we will see patterns that are not there. Thus, a preliminary aspect of any data analysis is to reorganize the data set in some way that makes it more convenient and conducive to the search for patterns. (One must take care, in such reorganizings, that the data are not distorted and that valuable information is not obscured or lost).

Such reorganization of the previously encoded and recorded data is most generally referred to as *data processing*. The rumpled TV detective may have made many notes on the backs of matchbooks and old grocery lists; before these scattered data can be of much use to him, they must somehow be brought together in a more orderly arrangement—perhaps only as scrawls on a blackboard. Or the social researcher has a closetful of questionnaires but cannot grasp the facts these contain until he or she can somehow reduce the bulkiness and sprawl of these recorded data into more manageable form.

Data processing—the reorganization of information to facilitate the search for patterns among data—has advanced enormously in our information society. Before writing and arithmetic, humans were stuck with only the crudest kinds of analysis because there was no way to reorganize data except in one's head. Number systems and writing led to a proliferation of ledgers, file folders, index cards, scroll libraries, and so on, which could be accumulated, cross-indexed, and reshuffled over long periods of time. During our own lifetimes, the development of electronics has produced such breakthroughs and holds such promise for information manipulation that many have dubbed our age postindustrial society or the information society.

Although electronic data processing has mushroomed to include the storage and retrieval of every kind of data to facilitate nearly every type of data analysis, it was invented in response to the needs of statistical analysis. The mechanical aspects of data analysis are extensively taught in texts on research methods and statistics. The creative aspects of analysis are given far less treatment, although they are probably more important in the long run to the development of knowledge and the history of mankind. Although the creative aspects of analysis, as of research in general, are much harder to teach, greater attention to these would be well worth the effort.

So what kind of analysis do we do? That depends on a number of factors. Partly it depends on the nature of the inquiry. If we need some quick answers, some crude quasi-statistical estimations may serve quite well. If we are exploring a relatively new area, or a new approach to a familiar area, a search for qualitative patterns may get us going. Because research is a more or less collective human endeavor, we or others can later do more exacting, extensive, and expensive quantitative studies. If we want to refine or verify some notions floating around, or some promising leads from pilot studies, we will probably want to go quantitative. For instance, a researcher might pick up hints of certain typical problems and adjustment patterns among single parents, then do a quasi-statistical pilot inquiry, and then seek funding for a full-fledged quantitative study. However, the sequence from qualitative to quasi-statistical to quantitative is not an inevitable one, nor is quantitative analysis necessarily better or more scientific than qualitative. Breakthroughs in all fields have often been new qualitative conceptualizations based upon fresh examinations of quantitative studies.

What kind of analysis we do also depends partly on our resources, since these determine size of sample, amount of data gathered, and so on. Given the nature of the inquiry, one does the best one can with what one has.

The state of the art, or degree of development, of the subject under investigation will also bear heavily on what kinds of analysis we can do. We are limited by how refined the concepts are for this area, how sophisticated are the measuring devices that exist, and the like. For example, we have no equivalent to the electron microscope in sociology. Nor do we have anything like the PET-scan to measure likelihood of repeat offenses among those arrested for the first time. There is plenty of work for anyone who wants to do research.

Whatever kinds of analysis we employ, it is patterns that we are after, because these lead us further along our trail of truth. Whatever patterns are found must now be evaluated.

CHAPTER

9

EVALUATION

If analysis considers what the data show, then *evaluation* is a consideration of what the data *mean*. We all go around interpreting the signs from our environment—someone's smile or frown, a slight rise in interest rates, a sudden cooling of the air. Such interpretations are carried out by assigning some theoretical or practical meanings to these signs, on the basis of our mental conceptions and our plans of action. The professional researcher is simply more objective and conscious about his or her evaluations and draws implications according to established rules.

In evaluation, we seek to discover what, if anything, has really been found out. We must interpret the meanings that the analyzed data have for our research concerns. What light do the results shed on our understanding of something?

Occasionally, we may undervalue or miss the significance of our data. An amateur collector may be unable to identify his or her latest catch and may merely assume that the guidebooks are incomplete, with the result that a previously unknown species of butterfly is lost to science. Many thousands of amateurs and professionals had previously stumbled over the same data that later led Newton to the laws of motion and Einstein to the theory of relativity. Incidents of this kind are a tragic undercurrent in the history of knowledge.

Much more often, however, both scientists and laymen attach too great a significance to their own data. The unusual case is taken for the typical: a few promising laboratory tests excite the medical researcher to conclude he is on the threshold of a cure. Or correlation is taken for causality: noting that delinquents tend to be poorly educated, a social researcher advocates new educational programs as a remedy for delinquency.

Because we have invested resources and our own self-regard in some inquiry, we tend to overvalue the fruits of that inquiry—the data as analyzed. Consequently, people everywhere tend to overgeneralize from improperly analyzed data that were perhaps poorly sampled and questionably reliable: "women are too emotional" or "people are against the benefit cuts." People tend to form fixed opinions from tiny bits of odd data and henceforth operate on the basis of them; they have one unpleasant experience in the swimming pool and may henceforth tell themselves (and their children, and their children's children), "Don't go near the water."

In each of these cases, a moment of honest and cool-headed evaluation of the likely worth of the data would lead these humans to concede that the slender reed of their data is too frail to sustain the weighty implications drawn from them. But in reality it is only the overeager scientists who are at all likely to undertake such a reappraisal. The skeptical "show me" attitude of the scientific community places a daily premium on the practice of evaluation. It is the element of Evaluation—not sampling, or measurement, or analysis—that by some accounts most sharply distinguishes professional research from everyday inquiry.

ELEMENT OF TRUSTWORTHINESS

How are the fruits of inquiry—the data as analyzed—reasonably evaluated and interpreted? One evaluative criterion is whether the data as analyzed constitute an answer to one of the research questions that animated and guided the inquiry. If so, then the data have at least some clear worth—they make some clear sense. If the data do not constitute an answer to one of the research questions, then we must ask: What questions do the data answer, or what new questions do they raise?

In either case, we will want to know how the data as analyzed fit into the framework of existing knowledge—a second aspect of the data making sense. On a pleasant morning, you read your backyard thermometer. If it says 75 degrees, you are not surprised and you take it for more or less fact. If it says 90 degrees, you are rather surprised, but by invoking such factors as low humidity and a nice breeze you can make sense enough of this reading to let it pass. However, if your thermometer says 147 degrees, either this is the hottest news since the Chicago fire or else there is something wrong with your thermometer, for such a result is implausible (makes no sense). The less expectable a result, the more extenuating circumstances we must invoke in our intepretation of it and the more cross-checks we demand on it. Startling results require a lot more confirmation to be accepted, while less verification is demanded of expected results. But, of course, the startling results are the ones most likely to push our wheel of collective human intelligence forward.

Results that are out of line with all other experience and our expectations are particularly interesting. The fact that sharks do not get cancer, or that local officials will not enforce drug laws in certain areas, or that a large number of the major thinkers in the Western world have expressed some belief in reincarnation, are anomalies or odd facts. Such findings may turn out to be (1) false in some important respect, (2) freakish oddities of little general significance, or (3) keys to potential revolutionary breakthroughs in our knowledge.

A third check on the meaningfulness of data as analyzed involves carefully weighing and considering their implications for theory and practice. The results of Robert Merton's reanalysis of data from the American soldier studies strongly showed the importance of reference groups in people's evaluations of themselves. The negative findings of the Mars landing expedition forced biologists to rethink the likely distribution of life forms. The implications for medical practice of Jenner's early experimentation with vaccination were quickly appreciated. Intelligible, plausible, and important implications of results enhance the significance of those results.

The analyzed data must, however, do more than make good sense or excite our interest. Results must be not only meaningful but *trustworthy* if they are to have much significance. A trustworthy result of obscure meaning tends in science to be more highly valued than a meaningful result of doubtful trustworthiness; facts are valued even when their implications are unclear. Thus, the fruits of an inquiry are also judged in large part by the soundness of the process by which they were generated.

But we must be careful here. Knowledge is sometimes obtained by the damndest means, and perfection in inquiry is as impossible to attain as in any other human endeavor. The presence of flaws, weaknesses, or limitations in a piece of research is not only inevitable, but it also does not necessarily mean that the inquiry has produced the wrong answer. Rust spots and crumpled fenders do not keep an automobile from being reliable transportation, although a faulty transmission or bad tires might. Deciding whether to trust the results of an inquiry is much like deciding whether to trust a person; we don't demand that the person has been absolutely right in everything he has done and said. Trust is always a bet, and trustworthiness is a matter of evidence and probability rather than proof.

Key factors in evaluation, then, are criteria and standards of trustworthiness for the interwoven elements of inquiry. Appropriate criteria have been described throughout the chapters of Part II. Research questions, for example, should be relevant and both definitely and empirically answerable. Samples should be adequate, unbiased, and representative. Data sets should be factual, accurate, relevant, and adequate. Measurements should be accurate, precise, reliable, and valid. Analysis of data should avoid both false positives and false negatives.

The degree to which all the elements of an inquiry meet the pertinent criteria is the prime measure of the trustworthiness of its results. Many of the preferred techniques of professional research permit objective measurement of the degree to which various criteria have been met. For example, probability sampling methods allow rather powerful assessment of the magnitude of sampling error, and objective measurement procedures permit similar assessment of measurement error. Statistical methods of data analysis make it possible to estimate and to control the likelihood of false negatives and false positives. Being able to assess rather objectively the degree to which an inquiry meets the criteria of trustworthiness is a prime factor in the superiority of professional research over ordinary inquiry.

But no study will meet these criteria completely; there will always be some degree of sampling error, measurement error, and the like. So, how closely must a study meet such criteria in order to be trustworthy? This is a problem of *standards*. What is good enough from the standpoint of one party may not be nearly good enough from the standpoint of another.

After all, standards are only guidelines for our betting on the correctness of study results. Establishing standards for a particular study must take into account what's at risk in this bet—what do we stand to lose if we're wrong in trusting these results? If our purpose in undertaking the inquiry is merely to satisfy our curiosity about the subject matter, our bet is a relatively light wager. But if we intend to take some action based upon the results of this study, the bet is more consequential. Being wrong about the results of engineering studies or medical lab tests may cost innocent lives, whereas in some other cases there is nothing more at stake than some transient embarrassment for appearing foolish. The urgency of having to make the bet is also a factor; can we afford to wait for more definitive information, or must be plunge ahead immediately on the basis of whatever results we've got? A closely related consideration is the existing state of knowledge; if very little is known, even poor information from this study would be a welcome addition, but if the state of the art is highly developed, only very accurate and precise results would be of much value.

Where the stakes are high, standards of trustworthiness are pegged at a high level of stringency also. Where the urgency is great, these standards may need to be relaxed substantially. But most human inquiry is undertaken not because we absolutely need to find something out but because we would like to do so. There is no great urgency and there is not a great deal at stake. The state of the art then tends to dominate in setting the level to which a study must meet the criteria of trustworthiness; more highly developed fields may conventionally require stringent limits on error caused by sampling and measurement, whereas less advanced fields hold rather relaxed standards.

ATTRIBUTES OF EVALUATOR

Although there are conventional criteria, standards, and guidelines for interpreting the worth and significance of analyzed data, evaluation remains a *creative* process that will never be reduced to any mechanical rote procedure. In order to draw implications from the analyzed data that are both meaningful and trustworthy, it is well for the evaluator to have (and improve) a number of attributes:

1. *A solid grounding in the work previously done in the subject area and related fields, from as many different approaches as possible.* This requires a good deal of training and homework, but it pays off handsomely and is one of the distinguishing

differences between the expert and the amateur. Without this depth and breadth of knowledge, the results of any study will appear only as isolated items to the evaluator. How would you interpret a trend of rising bond prices without a good background in financial markets and economics? What does a reversal in the long-standing decline in urban birth rates mean? What are the implications of a shift in the spectrum of a distant star? We don't have the answers to these questions either, because we are not knowledgeable in these fields. That is the point.

2. *Objectivity on the study, on oneself, and on one's self-involvement in the finding out project.* Whether the professional researcher is a nice person or not, and whatever you may think of his or her political views or taste in entertainment, one distinguishing mark of the real investigator (as opposed to the huckster) is brutal candor toward his or her own work. The pro agrees to play by the rules and, however arrogant he or she may be personally, has a degree of humility toward the research process that inspires personal integrity; the pro doesn't cheat on the results to favor some pet notion. These are the people who have given us all the advances in knowledge that are worth anything, and they'll be the ones who break the back of cancer and get us to the stars.

3. *Care and deliberation in arriving at one's interpretations.* The bases of the inferences are carefully identified, and the chains of reasoning are spelled out so that others can easily see (and disagree or reinterpret) them. It is entirely permissible for an inquirer to go far beyond his data in speculating on the nature of something, but he spells out explicitly how and why he is making such leaps. In ordinary life, such leaps beyond the data are simply made on some intuitive basis and then argumentatively defended. They may be right, of course, and often are, but the research elements are not available for cool examination by self or others.

4. *The fitting of the results into the context of the wider world (both theoretical and practical).* The ordinary persons is likely to be interested in some immediate application, such as "Will I get rained on?" or "What should I do with my $5,000?" The professional is after the big picture—regional and global weather patterns, or shifts in best investment opportunities as national economic factors change. He is out to capture a more universally applicable truth.

Perhaps the one most important thing you should know about evaluation is that evaluation is *not* simply an after-the-fact consideration that begins when the inquiry has been completed. Intelligent beings are always both perceiving and evaluating their environments. Evaluation is an interwoven element throughout the course of any inquiry: Does this research decision make sense? Is this research activity good enough? Should I go for something a little better here? Intelligent beings constantly monitor and appraise their own thoughts and actions. The problem is that ordinary inquiry is not consistently self-reflective and well-informed, and it tends to lack explicit criteria and standards for evaluation.

Evaluation always involves what is called extrapolation: going beyond the data to establish their meanings and implications. The professional researcher, having paid attention to the guidelines for each of the previous elements, is simply in a much stronger position from which to make such extrapolations. Evaluation is particularly that element through which our conceptual models are refined and perhaps enriched from our empirical dip into some slice of the environment. However, for the inquiry to contribute to our wheel of collective human understanding, there must be communication.

CHAPTER
10
COMMUNICATION

Each research element intertwines with every other element in the ongoing progression of an inquiry, as you have seen. Communication also pervades each step of the research process and therefore involves far more than an after-the-fact reporting of results. If we don't communicate, at least internally with ourselves, we don't investigate.

Ironically, communication is perhaps the most underrated and neglected element of the research process. Through communication, the researcher interchanges information and ideas with the rest of humanity in a series of ongoing give-and-take interactions. Any inquiry, no matter how private, is always influenced and guided by information and ideas we have received, directly or indirectly, from others. And we have seen, in the previous chapter, that the significance of any result depends on its fit within the structure of collectively accumulated knowledge. Private information, no matter how soundly derived, can never be considered knowledge, for knowledge is necessarily public to some degree. To count as knowledge, information must survive the tests and trials of collective selection. The wheel of research, as we have shown earlier, is the wheel of *collective* human intelligence.

Looking backward over the other elements, we begin to see the vital part played by communication in our quest. Questions are posed on the basis of the cultural framework and background information communicated to the inquirer. Communication also has special connections to the element of resources, because obtaining resources almost always involves negotiations, requests, or proposals. And so on through to the element of evaluation; sharing information and ideas with others is our most effective means for minimizing every kind of blunder and blinder. Also, assessing the full meaning and implications of our eventual results is, in the final analysis, carried out through a communication interchange with the rest of humanity. Expending limited resources to obtain information that will not be shared is, from the viewpoint of human history, a waste. Private information is wasted information because it robs others of what might have been a valuable resource for their own inquiries and lives.

TWO-WAY AND CIRCULAR INTERCHANGES

Most textbooks on research methods seriously shortchange the student by a one-sided treatment of the communication element, emphasizing only the techniques for reporting research. The reality is that communication is a two-way street, an *interchange* of information and ideas—taking in as well as giving out.

The most important two-way communication is that in which the investigator continuously confers with himself or herself throughout the entire research process. Social psychologists have long pointed out that through such internal conversations intelligent beings monitor and appraise their own thoughts and actions. Guided by the rules and routines we have been examining, the researcher monitors, refines, evaluates, edits, revises, and criticizes his or her own work at each stage of the inquiry. This is a healthy process that helps to steer a safe course between arrogance and naiveté.

Such internal conversations can draw upon the research guidelines throughout each phase of the inquiry to produce more and better results with less floundering and effort. "Does additional information already exist on this subject? Where? What does some colleague think or know about this? Is my question answerable with what data I can get? What else do these data mean? Can others comprehend what the hell I'm saying? I think something else is going on that I'm missing." And so on, throughout the investigation.

Most inquiries are, however, not solo endeavors but involve some help from others; most research is, to some degree, a team effort. Critical discussions and brainstorming sessions with one's teammates or collaborators are a major influence in shaping the form and directions of an inquiry. In such communications, the co-workers apply to one another and to the project as a whole all those guidelines discussed in previous chapters, bringing up additional background data, suggesting promising leads, pointing out weaknesses, and so on.

Often, we undertake an inquiry on behalf of, or with an eye toward, some second party who needs or wants information. Commonly, such a second party is underwriting or paying for the investigation, or at least paying our salaries. Such funders, or providers of resources, may be patrons (such as a private foundation or other granting agency) or clients who contract for knowledge (such as a business firm or private individual). The investigator is always obliged to listen respectfully to the ideas, questions, and suggestions of any patron or client, and also to report back to them at reasonable intervals.

Beyond these immediate circles there are always other independent investigators (colleagues) who have been and are pursuing similar research questions. The fruits of their efforts afford us a launching pad for our own investigations; we see farther because we stand on the shoulders of those who have been there before us. Any inquirer would be wise to listen to anything these fellow voyagers might have to say. Also, the first testing of the conclusions of an inquiry usually involves subjecting the findings to the informed judgments of these colleagues. Such judgments will be objectively evaluated, through internal communication, by the wise investigator. Science—our wheel of collective human intelligence—is actually carried forward by an international community of colleagues who mutually evaluate, verify, and refine the work done in every subject area. This international scientific community is subject to collective blunders and blinders of its own, such as inertia, culture lag, and tunnel vision, but is the most stable and trustworthy long-run source of progress yet evolved by mankind.

Often, too, there are special publics of select laymen and professional practitioners with a particular interest in the topic of one's investigation. For example, practicing social workers have a keen interest in sociological researches on the family, youth culture, rape victims, and so on. Also, congressmen and their staffs will often eagerly ingest the results of public opinion studies. The collective interest and experience of such special publics often inspire and facilitate the efforts of an investigator, and their excitement and enthusiasm for reports of new knowledge are always gratifying and often sobering.

Finally, there is the general public, which also has a right to know. The common sense of the man in the street is a major check on the significance and intelligibility of what we have learned. In turn, many of the assumptions and interests that provoke and shape our research questions derive from the common sense views vested in our native culture. There is also a communication loop here, in that research results sometimes filter back to influence and change the lives of the populace at large.

Thus, these various circles of communication (depicted in Figure 7) play somewhat different roles in the research process. As one moves outward from the center in Figure 7, the frequency and the centrality—but not necessarily the importance—of communication declines.

The interrelationships of communication flows among these various circles of audiences are complex and fascinating. For one thing, there is a greater or lesser time lag as one moves outward, so that the circles closest in are most in the know on any subject. For example, the research community is always more up to date than the community of practitioners in a profession like dentistry or criminology. Similarly, the general public may be influenced by research results long before they understand or even hear much about the inner circles, as was the case with the development of the electronic chip or the use of monetarist fiscal theories by our government. Findings may have great practical significance for the outer circles but be of

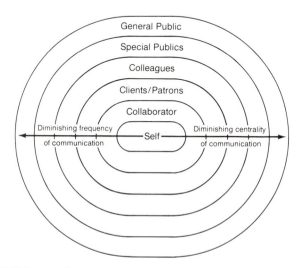

FIGURE 7. The Investigator's Circles of Communication

little theoretical interest, or they may have great theoretical importance but little immediate practical application, so that the outer
circles become impatient and stingy with their support, as with the
space program. A whole social psychology of research could be built
upon the interrelations among these various audiences, with communication (or the lack of it) being the key.

ONGOING COMMUNICATION

Because textbooks treat communication largely as a matter of reporting the eventual results of an inquiry, these treatments imply that
communication is what one does after everything else has been completed. In practice, communication is an important element throughout the process of inquiry—before, during, and after—as shown in
Figure 8.

Before an inquiry even begins, direct and indirect inputs from
others provide the background information that both inspires and
frames the inquiry. The investigator then submits a research proposal;
in ordinary inquiry, this may only amount to a casual and tentative
mention to close confidants, but in professional research it usually
represents a formal and highly developed document submitted to
some qualified body. In either case, such a proposal may also include

FIGURE 8. The Spiral of Communication Within an Inquiry

some request for resources and always solicits some evaluative response from others. This evaluative response, or feedback, often leads the investigator to revise his or her plans, or at the extreme, to drop them altogether.

During an inquiry, the investigator periodically reports to others on how the inquiry is progressing. Within the research team (self and collaborators), such reports most often take the form of conversational discussions, but sometimes involve formal oral reports in staff meetings or internal working papers and memos. Clients or patrons often demand some type of periodic progress reports, and preliminary progress reports may be made to external colleagues as presentations to scholarly conventions, or quite informally. Special publics, too, may request interim information, and even the general public may be interested in hearing how the study is coming along. Progress reports of any kind delivered to nearly any of these audiences inspire some sort of return communication or feedback that influences the continuing conduct of the investigation.

As the research wraps up, there are final reports to any and all of the circles of audiences. Here is where the inquiry is most likely to enter the stream of collective information and, perhaps, the culture at large. Here, too, is where the results are likely to be stored in some manner for later retrieval to form the background information of future investigators. Thus, our wheel has come forward a turn.

INPUTS AND OUTPUTS

The input side of the communication process receives little attention in textbooks on research. They rarely advise the inquirer as to how, when, or from where he should elicit and collect various types of communications from others in the course of his inquiry. When such advice is offered, it most often applies to obtaining backgrounding and almost never to obtaining critical feedback. Perhaps the most important communication skill in the research process is that of interpreting, evaluating, and using feedback received from others. Few of us enjoy criticism, but the successful investigator is one who has learned how to constructively use—rather than deflect or discount—the critical responses of others.

Even though these skills of critical reading and critical listening are seldom actually taught in research courses, many textbooks on research do at least emphasize that communication outputs need to be sensitively responsive to the specific context of communication. That is, they emphasize that the how (form) and the what (content) of any communication output should take into account the who, when, and why of that communication (audience, occasion, and purpose).

We have already seen, in Figure 10–2, how the content of the investigator's communication outputs varies over time as a function of his or her changing purposes. Early outputs (proposals) emphasize ideas, plans, and rationales and are framed to seek support. In mid-course, outputs (working papers and progress reports) emphasize preliminary information and the handling of operational difficulties and are framed to maintain support. Later outputs (final reports) emphasize findings, interpretations, and evaluations and are framed to influence knowledge.

Moreover, the content of any such communication needs to be further tailored to the resources and interests of a specific audience. Some audiences will be prepared and motivated to absorb any and all details of the research. More often, a particular audience will be interested in only select aspects of the research; the wise communicator then does not lose his message in a morass of extraneous details. The tailoring of content must also take account of the resources of the audience; if, for example, the statistical sophistication of the audience is minimal, then statistical details on the topic of interest should be omitted or translated into some alternative type of information such as visual displays.

Form, too, must adapt to the purpose, occasion, and audience of communication. The medium of communication is one key aspect of form. Oral communication may be more effective under certain circumstances, but written communication more effective under others. And in the late twentieth century, a wide variety of audiovisual media are also available—movies, videotapes, computer graphics, and the like. These, in turn, open the possibility of mixed-media presentations, such as an oral presentation woven around a series of slides.

With so many circles of audiences, it is not surprising that a great deal of the communication regarding any inquiry is indirect. For example, a research team may report to its funding agency the results of a child abuse study; this report is seen by other professionals, who mention it to a newspaper reporter, who gets it and writes an item about its results in his column. This item is read by a PTA officer, who tells her fellow members about it. The PTA chapter may then request that the funding agency launch further studies along some particular direction of interest to its members. Or, during a recession, large segments of the populace may lobby for a reduction in the space program because they do not perceive its benefits.

The quality of communication in such indirect chains is often quite poor, with major distortions and omissions sometimes occurring all along the line. Thus, a thirty-second capsule on the evening news, summarizing a five-year study, may leave much to be desired.

Another point is that it is often difficult to break through to communicate with the wider circle of audiences. All audiences are limited in their willingness and ability to receive communications, and so erect barriers and filters. Certain segments of the communication net may also be more or less automatically denied communication access to other segments, for all kinds of reasons, including especially the blinders discussed in Chapter 2. Orthodox medicine has turned a largely deaf ear for the findings of, say, chiropractic and nutrition until quite recently.

The inquirer wishing to communicate his results must bear in mind such aspects of indirect communication.

FAILINGS IN COMMUNICATION

As with every other element in the research process, the element of communication is strained by the inevitable fact that any human being's experience is both limited and selective. Every inquiry suffers from some failings in communication, on both the input and the output sides.

Even in the Information Society of today, where we are all awash in a swelling tide of communications, the information an investigator can take in and make use of is rather limited. One never has enough backgrounding or feedback, in part because of one's limited resources and in part because one derives this information from a limited range of sources. But selectivity is often more injurious, as the investigator relies too heavily on certain sources and hence receives a skewed or biased set of inputs. The most common instance of this is when the researcher gets virtually all his backgrounding from his own field but only slight and haphazard backgrounding from related fields. Even within one's own field one may hold some partisan position, resulting in further selectivity of what one does and does not look at.

There are some similar problems on the output side. Reporting of the inquiry is always in a digested form where the months-long work of a dozen researchers may, for instance, be condensed into a few pages of summary. This calls for caution to not distort the picture in the act of condensing and not to omit important messages. Also, the audiences reached tend always to be limited and skewed, as we have seen.

The research community at large has evolved guidelines for this element, too, to overcome these input and output problems. Reportage formats have been standardized, for example. Input failings will almost inevitably show up in this system of standardized reportage, and revisions will be called for or the communication will be rejected by the professional audiences.

In ordinary life, many people share their perceptions of the world and their hard-won evaluations with family and friends, and perhaps a few others, but the vast majority let it go at that. How much knowledge has been lost in this manner is incalculable. The professional researcher strives to broadcast his or her results and inferences in such a way that a public record of how the inquiry was done and what was found is created. In terms of our wheel of collective human intelligence, a crucial element in the research game is to record the project in such a manner that it can be retrieved, examined, re-evaluated, and used by others. It then becomes part of our common heritage.

PART
III

MODES OF
SOCIAL RESEARCH

As we have seen, each of the eight key elements in research contains within itself numerous options. However, the research process is definitely not like ordering from a Chinese menu—any option from Column 1, any from Column 2, and so on. All these options lend themselves to only a few effective combinations—the proven, major modes of social research. Each of these modes is a general logic, harnessing the eight elements in just such a way as to answer one very broad but definitely limited class of research questions. Nearly all effective social research follows one of four major modes—secondary research/secondary analysis, survey research, participant observation, and experiments.

Each of these major research modes can be likened to a highly developed and internally consistent *style* of cooking, like French versus Japanese cooking, or stovetop versus microwave cooking. Each can produce a wide but definitely bounded range of dishes, all of which are distinctively compatible. The strength of these traditional styles derives from the fact that the separate elements—the kinds of ingredients, the kinds of tools, the techniques of preparation, blending, and cooking—have selectively evolved together into some jointly coherent logic of cooking. The separate elements fit together well, working in a mutually supportive fashion.

And so it is in the major modes of social research. Within such a mode, or style, the type of research question has coevolved with certain options in sampling, data collection, measurement, analysis, and so on. Envision the web of Figure 9 as being something like a bicycle wheel, where all the lines represent spokes of that wheel and all the nodes represent the various elements of research. If there is a lack of fit between any two elements, such as qualitative data and statistical analysis, we can think of that spoke as being missing. The more spokes missing, the weaker the wheel of research. The researcher must make every effort to ensure the fit between each pair of elements.

To take the analogy one step farther, we could consider the degree of such fit; the greater the fit between two elements, the longer the spoke. If some spokes are then much longer than others, the wheel of research is thrown out of round and will roll along only bumpily, if at all. The researcher must also, then, make every effort to ensure an overall balance in the fits between element pairs.

By choosing to employ one of the well-developed major modes of social research, the researcher is more or less assured of having a workable wheel. His responsibilities then amount to checking to make sure no spokes happen to be missing and that the wheel is not too far out of balance.

Each of the four modes of research is continually employed by all human beings, at least in rudimentary form, so none of us are strangers to them. A motorist finds and checks an existing map for routes through the desert, instead of needlessly repeating the original explorations of the mapmaker. Newspaper ads are surveyed for jobs or housing price ranges or grocery sales. Participant observation is universally employed in scouting for places to live and for new personal relationships. A homemaker experiments with a new

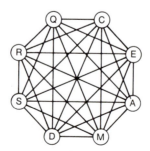

FIGURE 9. The Web of Research Elements

product, and an infant experiments with different body movements.

- Secondary research/analysis——"look it up."
- Survey research——"ask around to compare."
- Participant observation——"hang around to check it out."
- Experiment——"try it and see."

CHAPTER

11

SECONDARY RESEARCH AND SECONDARY ANALYSIS

Without secondary research we would all be condemned to reinventing arithmetic and rediscovering fire on our own all over again. The vast bulk of anyone's data comes second hand or hundredth hand. Each child enters a world and a society that is already rich with a multitude of answers on a vast array of subjects. There is now probably no one left on this planet who is so isolated that he or she is not at least tenuously connected with the wheel of collective human intelligence. A person would progress little above the level of a brute if he or she had to rediscover all these accumulated understandings on their own. Also, as we have seen, any original inquiry is launched from the backgrounding of previous investigations. For example, think of the uncountable accumulations of inventions, researches, and understandings represented in an ordinary world atlas, including the census figures of hundreds of countries, the mappings of the ocean floor, world temperature and climate maps, and the photos of the planet viewed from space.

But beyond all these points, secondary research is a major mode of research in its own right. That is, it is not always necessary for an inquirer to directly generate new data in order to empirically answer the research questions posed. Often, in this Information Society, the appropriate data already exist and may even have already been appropriately analyzed. If both of these conditions hold, the inquirer need only look up the answer to the research question; this process of looking up the answer is known as *secondary research* (or library research, a process to which most students already have been introduced). If, however, appropriate data exist but have not yet been appropriately analyzed, the inquirer need only borrow the data and perform the necessary analysis of them; this process of borrowing data is known as *secondary analysis.* Both of these processes, however, involve each of the eight basic elements we have examined in Part II.

The word *secondary* in these two phrases in no way implies that secondary research or analysis is less important or less noble. It means only that the inquirer did not, directly and at first hand, collect the data. On the basis of our discussion in Chapter 4 of resources as an element in the research process, secondary research/analysis should be the inquirer's first choice as a mode of social research, because it conserves scarce resources that might otherwise be spent in collecting data that are already available.

Secondary research is the mode most often employed in everyday life. We check our street map to find an acquaintance's house, we pursue our interest in Australia or chess through reading books on the subject, we query friends when we need a lawyer or health specialist. Or we consult the yellow pages. For professional practitioners, this is also the major mode in which professional journals, workshops, and consultations with colleagues provide the bulk of the updating on new developments and techniques. For instance, a social worker would be most likely to find out about the success of a victim self-help group through published reports or a seminar. The professional researcher thoroughly checks into what has been done before proceeding with a new inquiry. And as stored information accumulates in our time, a growing number of studies are based in part or wholly on the secondary analysis of already existing data.

The questions posed in secondary research can be any of the types discussed in Chapter 3: descriptive, explanatory, or verificational. "What highway leads to Barstow? Why do my gums keep getting infected? Is Marsten College fully accredited?" Sometimes these questions are of an immediate practical nature, in which the person needs some answer in order to handle a situation. The person needs to rent an apartment or buy a stereo set, or the boss wants a plane reservation to New York. Commonly, however, the person will simply have a curiosity to know about some subject, perhaps with the yet unfocused intention to pursue that subject or develop some future plan of action with the information. In such cases, there is often a progression over time from secondary research to one or more of the other research modes.

But even in secondary research, resourcefulness is a major factor in the success or failure of any attempt at looking up an answer to a research question, as anyone who has ever tried a hand at library research knows. Material resources are certainly vital, including not only the size and quality of the library holdings to which you can gain access but also time, personnel, and technology. Library research can be a time-consuming process, particularly when your own library must send off for materials from other libraries. If you must do all the combing through books, journals, directories, bibliographies, and indexes yourself, the expenditure of time is especially clear; a team project can often complete the process of inquiry within a shorter span of calendar time. Technological aids, such as microfiche readers and computerized search procedures, can both broaden and speed the process. Without adequate material resources of all these kinds, you may not be able to locate a satisfactory answer to your question even though it exists in a quite retrievable place.

In today's emerging Information Society, the ability to locate and extract specific data grows in importance in every field. In one view, each person draws upon an *information net* or interlaced grid of input information sources for the answers to most of his or her questions. Extending this net and learning the craft of gaining answers from it are key parts of the training for professionals in most fields, from medicine to investments and real estate to the social sciences.

For both amateurs and professionals, there are two main problems with data from such information nets. First, the secondary data are almost always boiled down a great deal. This can be handy because the data are predigested and summarized for fast and easy use. But we are at the mercy of condensations carried out by others; details valuable for our own purposes may have been lost in the compacting. Others selected the importances and unimportances for *their* purposes, which might differ widely from ours.

Second, in such condensations it is often difficult to distinguish data and valid inferences from mere opinions, personal viewpoints, and the like. Take such statements as "Zelditch is a good doctor" or "There is rising opposition to the new tax program." What is the actual basis for these assertions? This is a special problem with traveler's journals, documentary footage, commentaries, case study folders, magazine articles, and newspaper accounts. Often it is hard to disentangle the author's findings from the author's value judgments.

Information nets usually combine both material and human resources. Strictly human resources involve the skills of those contacted, such as a reference librarian, and the organizational, interpersonal, and intellectual skills of the inquirer. If the answers sought are embedded in technical or foreign language sources, these skill levels become even more crucial.

Given any particular skill level and the ability to get others to help, persistence is the critical factor determining whether the investigator gets an answer and how good that answer will be. Again and again, in every field, the persistent inquirer triumphs while his or her less tenacious fellows fail. Because knowledge correlates with success, such triumphs may mean much more than the simple satisfaction of some idle curiosity.

As is true with every major research mode, there are those who specialize in secondary research and analysis. The volume of facts such people can quickly lay their hands on is sometimes awesome— to the point that they themselves become a major resource through the fruits of their own work and through the help they can provide others.

But most important in secondary research are environmental resources. The body of existing information may not, in fact, contain within it the answer we are seeking. Or the political climate may be such that although the necessary information exists in retrievable form, it may be considered proprietary, classified, or secret information to which we are not entitled.

The count of our resources, together with the nature of our research question, will largely shape the element of sampling—that is, where we look (and don't look) for our answer. We may be limited to American sources, or at least to English language sources; we may be limited to popular rather than professional or highly technical sources; we may be limited to the holdings of our local library. Here our own knowledge and skills in looking up information can make a great deal of difference; we can readily become considerably more expert at broadening and deepening the population of sources within which we look by reading one of the many helpful guidebooks to library research (see Suggested Readings at the end of this book).

Data collection then amounts to the process of finding the needed information within the sampled sources, that is, recognizing, encoding, and storing information that meets the criteria of relevance, factualness, accuracy, and adequacy. Such borrowed data may need to be recombined in some novel way, involving us in a process of measurement. Inevitably, when more than one datum is required, as in the case of finding some pattern or progression of events, we move automatically into the element of analysis.

Evaluation involves us in two tasks. First, the trustworthiness of the borrowed data must be assessed; if key data about the data are missing, we are left in a best-guess position regarding their worth. Second, the borrowed data must be held up to our own research question to examine their fit and figure out their implications. If the data fit the frame of inquiry and give us our answers, we're home free. If not, the secondary data may still shed some light on our subject and perhaps some clues regarding the directions we should next pursue. There is thus often an A to B to C sort of reference trail in secondary research, much resembling a children's treasure hunt game.

The secondary research we have been discussing so far is basically skilled information retrieval. Most professional specialists can carry out fast, deep information retrievals in their own fields—in fact, this is part of the skill one develops in becoming a pro in some area. Beyond this, we enter the level of full secondary analysis of previously collected data. There are two major forms of secondary analysis. The first involves combining together various existing data to bear upon some research questions newly posed. Bits of information may be pieced together from different sources—a fact from here, an opinion from there, an observation from some practitioner, another fact from over yonder. As the investigator puts these bits together, he or she may come up with a new picture, a new slant, some refinement of existing conceptual models, or a breakthrough. Sometimes this involves the recombining of old, semi-lost data or concepts with new emerging results, as in some current nutritional breakthroughs or recent research into humanity's beginnings on this planet.

The second broad form of secondary analysis involves the reanalysis of sets of data that have been systematically collected, analyzed, evaluated, and stored according to all the research guidelines we have been examining in previous chapters. Often, such data sets have been conveniently archived in some central and specialized repository* or published in one of the several important factbooks or data reports (such as the reports of the U.S. Bureau of the Census).†

Often, a set of good data are gathered for one purpose, so that a new researcher can come along and reanalyze the same data for different purposes, perhaps using newly developed techniques. Or some original, professionally processed data can be looked at newly in light of additional findings that have since emerged elsewhere.

The major advantage of secondary analysis is its incredible cost-effectiveness. One can pursue inquiries with others' existing data that would be impossible if one had to go out and collect all the data oneself.

Also, certain types of comparative studies are only possible through use of secondary data, for instance, comparative cross-cultural studies, or the tracing of population shifts in opinion over decades. The potential of such comparative studies is only beginning to be realized as retrievable data accumulate in our modern age.

Secondary inquiry, of either the look it up or the reanalysis type, involves all the elements of any inquiry. All the rules and routines apply. Empirically answerable questions must be posed, resources must be marshalled and deployed, a sample slice must be found that reflects the shape of the whole being investigated, reliable data must be obtained and measurements constructed. Proper analysis must be performed to find the patterns that exist in the data, these results must be evaluated carefully, and communications must occur if the inquiry is to become part of our communal human history.

Undoubtedly the most vital element in both secondary research and in secondary analysis is the element of evaluation, for here it must do double duty. At the first level, the inquirer must searchingly evaluate those sources on which he has chosen to depend. How meaningful and how trustworthy is the answer one has looked up

---

*A convenient list of such archival respositories is provided in Catherine Hakim, *Secondary Analysis in Social Research: A Guide to Data Sources and Methods with Examples* (London: George Allen & Unwin, 1982), pp. 165–168. See also *Directory of Social Science Data Archives*.

†U.S. Department of Commerce, *Statistical Abstract of the United States* (Washington, D.C.: U.S. Government Printing Office, various years). See also P. G. Carter, *U.S. Census Data for Political and Social Research: A Resource Guide* (Washington, D.C.: American Political Science Association, 1976).

through secondary research? How trustworthy is the data set one has borrowed for secondary analysis?

Then, at a second level, the inquirer must carefully evaluate his or her own process of inquiry—the separate and combined quality of one's own questions, resources, sampling, data collection, measurement, analysis, and so on. Most critically, one needs to evaluate the skill and care with which one has carried out that first-level evaluation (of the sources on which one has chosen to depend).

The importance of secondary research and secondary analysis to the wheel of collective human intelligence is so clearcut that we state the following general rule of thumb for all human inquiry: First, try secondary research; if no satisfactory answer to the research question results, then try secondary analysis; if a satisfactory answer still has not been found, try primary research.

CHAPTER

12

SURVEY RESEARCH

Almost all of us have at some time been a subject of survey research, but few people have a very clear idea of what this research mode actually is. For example, survey research is not identical to interview and questionnaire research; any method of data collection from observation to content analysis can and has been used in survey research. Furthermore, survey research is not confined to studies of individuals; the subjects of survey research could equally as well be families, cities, business firms, police departments, or even monkeys or apples. One could, for example, survey neighborhoods in different cities in an attempt to see what factors led to high crime rates.

Survey research is actually a general *logic of research* that assumes only a certain way of conceptualizing the subject matter under study, and certain basic aims of inquiry.

Survey research is an appropriate mode of inquiry whenever it makes good sense to conceptualize what's being studied as essentially *a distinct population of basically similar objects.* For instance, a beach could be viewed as a population of grains of sand; a city could be thought of as a population of inhabitants or of buildings; and a church congregation could be viewed as a population of members. In all such cases, the component objects are thought to be of the same fundamental sort but differ from one another in certain fairly stable characteristics. Congregation members, for example, might differ from one another in their opinions about abortion or their attitudes toward the Old Testament, and grains of sand might differ from one another in coloration, size, and shape.

One way of getting at how one beach differs from another beach would be to compare the distributions of coloration, size, and shape in the two populations of sand grains. Differences in one or more of these statistical distributions might go a long way toward explaining certain gross differences between the two beaches in appearance or behavior. For example, because large grains are not easily blown by winds, the fact that only one of the beaches has sand dunes could easily be explained by showing that these beaches differ in their average size of sand grain. The basic aims of survey research are, in fact, to *statistically describe* and *statistically explain* the variability of certain features among those objects comprising some population (or populations).

Although this is not the proper place to begin to explain the subject of statistics, we should at least explain what is meant by statistical description and statistical explanation. *Statistical description* is nothing more than quantitatively summarizing a large number of empirical measurements—for example, how many of our measured sand grains are 100 microns in diameter, how many are 150 microns, 200 microns, and so on. How often any of these sizes occurred (frequencies) could be expressed as percentages of the total number of grains, or depicted by various lengths of bars in a pictorial chart. More compact summaries take the form of averages (together with measures of how accurately any particular average summarizes all the data). More complex descriptive statistics may summarize measurements of more than one variable at a time, such as how closely the peaks and valleys of one variable mirror those of another variable, or correlate. The phrase *survey research* calls to mind the work of a surveyor, who maps out the height and shape of the peaks and valleys of some particular landscape. We might, for instance, compare the distributions of opinions about abortion among Catholics, Protestants, and Jews to better comprehend the social geography of opinion.

Statistical explanation is the attempt to demonstrate that the peaks and valleys of one set of measured variables can be predicted mathematically from knowledge of some second set of measured variables. For example, we might find that high resident turnover in neighborhoods is highly correlated with crime rates, or that job absenteeism is much lower in corporations that give bonuses for consecutive days on the job. A great deal of market research is of the survey form: which ad or packaging sells more of the product? Today, an ever-increasing number of organizations of all kinds are engaged in survey research. They seek both statistical descriptions and statistical explanations, because this mode has proved its value in both science and practical affairs.

The general logic of survey research imparts a distinctive *style* or flavor to the research process, by largely determining, both separately and collectively, the shape taken by each of the eight basic elements of inquiry as they work together in support of that particular logic.

Let us begin with the element of *questions.* Every research question, like any other type of question, makes certain presuppositions about the world and our knowledge of it. For instance, a religious question might presuppose a spiritual nature of the universe and the sacredness of certain holy scriptures, whereas an empirical question presupposes the "reality" of events in the environment. The presuppositions of some, but not all, research questions are compatible with the type of world view fundamental to survey research: that many phenomena can be broken down into a population of component objects of one type that vary from one another in certain fairly stable characteristics. Furthermore, the presuppositions of some research questions are compatible with the basic aims of survey research, whereas others are not. For example, questions such as "What are the voters' current attitudes toward Reaganomics?" or "What are the average housing costs in various regions of the country?" lend themselves immediately to the survey research mode.

Similarly, survey research generally requires certain types and amounts of human, material, and environmental *resources.* Obviously one must have the material resources to carry out an adequate sampling and data gathering enterprise. Human resources are also necessary in larger amounts than for some other research modes. And finally, the environment must be such that the appropriate data can be elicited and extracted, which may involve some access problems and necessary negotiations. If one has an appropriate kind of research question and the appropriate resources, one might then adopt the logic of survey research in shaping the remaining elements of the research process.

Sampling, for example, becomes quite central and exacting in survey research, because the very subject matter of the study has been fundamentally conceptualized as a distinct population in the precise sense of Chapter 5, and because the basic aims of survey research are to statistically describe and explain variability within or between populations. Controlling sampling error thus becomes an overriding concern in survey research. Of course, sampling error can be eliminated by studying the entire population; survey research that studies the entire population is called a census survey, in contrast to the vastly more common sample surveys that attempt to characterize an entire population through close study of a carefully derived sample of cases. Researchers have become so skilled at this that the opinions and behaviors of entire populations can be successfully mapped through exploring only a minute fraction of the membership.

Survey *data* may be obtained through the use of virtually any of the many methods of data gathering, as noted earlier. Although the logic of survey research does not dictate the method by which data are to be obtained, it does dictate the manner or style in which data are obtained. That is, the basic aim of making statistical comparisons within a population of fundamentally similar objects necessarily produces within survey research a heavy emphasis on the systematic collection (rather than more casual gathering) of data. If the day-to-day procedures of data collection are allowed to vary at all from case to case, the resulting differences in the data obtained might masquerade as (or obscure) actual differences in the relevant characteristics being studied. For this reason, survey research takes great pains to *standardize* every step and aspect of data collection. Data are evoked in a uniform manner, selected in a uniform manner, encoded and recorded in a uniform manner.

Given such standardized data collection and the statistical aims of survey research, it follows that *measurement* will tend to be exacting and as numerical as possible. Measurement error serves to compound sampling error, so the drive to control the size of measurement error is the major impulse behind the standardization of data collection procedures.

Similarly, because the basic aims of survey research are statistical in character, *analysis* of data takes the form of quantitative (that is, truly statistical) rather than qualitative analysis. But unlike other quantitative styles of research, survey analysis relies centrally on correlational methods of statistical analysis. That is, in survey research we find relationships between measured variables, such as older people being more anti-abortion than younger people, or unemployment rates being far higher among black youths than white youths. Statistical explanations that employ these correlational methods do not necessarily constitute causal explanations. Considerable substantive and statistical expertise is required to determine whether a correlation between two variables is in fact due to any causal connection between them, but enormous advances have been made in this respect over the past two decades.

The element of *evaluation* in survey research distinctively emphasizes the control of sampling error. Concern for the control of measurement error is only slightly secondary and is highly visible in the somewhat compulsive drive to standardize every facet of data collection, measurement, and analysis. A hallmark of survey research is the importance placed on pretesting every procedure throughout the research process to guarantee the objectivity of the research plans and the comparability of data. Evaluating the *meaning* of the survey results involves filling in the statistical descriptive picture of the target population and also some clues (through the relationships found among variables) to the reasons for the profiles found. Often, the results are compared with data from other surveys of such populations in exploring the implications of the inquiry. Such comparison with earlier, similar surveys may reveal significant shifts in attitudes or behavior patterns. This is how we discover trends in unemployment rates, changes in the age composition of the populace, shifts in public opinion on current issues, changes in average sexual attitudes and behaviors, and the like.

Communication, too, takes a somewhat distinctive form in survey research. Like every major mode of social research, it has its own traditional formats for reporting an inquiry that in good part reflect the distinctive profile of concerns that dominate the element of evaluation in survey research. For example, these formats call for an unusually detailed accounting of every facet of the sampling process and of response rates. The communication of results to broader audiences is done through summaries of statistical descriptions and statistical explanations. These are increasingly picked up and further summarized by the mass media in the form of brief news spots.

As we noted earlier, the rudiments of the survey mode are commonly practiced by the ordinary layman. When we shop around for better grocery prices or a better auto service, we are employing this mode. A comparison of such efforts with the discussion of professional survey research points up the crucial differences: (1) in everyday life we are usually looking for a specific practical truth, such as "Overstep Auto Service gives us the best tune-up for the money," whereas the professional seeks a more universal, broadly applicable understanding, such as that cars which get regular tune-ups have a 30 percent higher value on their first resale; (2) the systematic, objective approach of the professional has it all over the haphazard, half-hearted inquiries of the amateur for reliability, validity, and scope of results.

Please note that anyone can improve his or her results with this mode in everyday life by simply: being a little more thoughtful and objective in applying each of the research elements; framing clear, answerable questions; being resourceful; sampling a bit more broadly and representatively; getting some decent data rather than mere hearsay; honestly analyzing and evaluating whatever is found, while keeping one eye out for blunders and blinders all along the line.

MEASURING POPULATION CHANGE

In the vast majority of survey research studies, measurements are made on characteristics of a population at a single point in time (cross-sectional research) rather than at several times (longitudinal research). Study of the same population over time permits the detection and analysis of change.

Several general designs for longitudinal survey research are well known. Trend studies examine some general population, such as American voters, by studying a separate sample at each time-point, with little if any overlap in membership; differences between sample results indicate change in population characteristics. But because different individuals are studied each time, one cannot learn whether any individual has changed in his or her characteristics. And because a general population of this type may experience considerable turnover in membership (old voters dying or dropping out, with new members entering constantly), even changes in population characteristics may be caused only by turnover and not by changes in any individuals.

Cohort studies are somewhat more informative in these respects, because they examine a more bounded population (such as "persons born in 1950") in which turnover is not possible. That is, although members of such a population may die, they can never be replaced by new members, because the world is no longer able to create any more "persons born in 1950." But like trend studies, cohort studies examine separate (generally nonoverlapping) samples. Differences between sample results thus indicate changes in population characteristics that cannot be attributed to turnover and must be the result of changes in individual characteristics; however, because of nonoverlapping samples, cohort studies cannot tell us which kinds of individuals are changing and which are not.

To find out that kind of fact requires a panel study, in which a single sample of individuals is examined at several points in time. Differences between sample results then indicate changes in population characteristics that cannot be attributed to turnover and also permit determination of which kinds of individuals are and are not changing.

True longitudinal studies of these three types are relatively expensive and necessarily long in completion time. Yet the interest in detecting and explaining change is often very great. Therefore, survey researchers sometimes resort to simulated longitudinal research, in which a cross-sectional study collects not only current data but also retrospective data, even though the limitations of such an approach are well known.

The survey mode, in all its forms, has proved its worth in forwarding our collective understanding of the world, both in everyday living and in professional social research. However, when survey research does not fit our inquiry, our situation, or our resources, we can turn to other major modes of primary research that may better serve our needs.

CHAPTER

13

PARTICIPANT OBSERVATION

Very different from the style of survey research is participant observation. This mode of research, classically exemplified by the work of the lone anthropologist living among an isolated people, involves some amount of genuine social interaction in the field with the subjects of the study, considerable direct observation of relevant events, some formal and a great deal of informal interviewing, some systematic counting, some collection of documents and artifacts, and open-endedness in the directions the study takes as it progresses.

Recently, this mode has been widely adopted by newsmen and magazine feature writers because it can deliver an in-depth picture of some slice of social reality that is hard to match through other modes. Thus, we learn about life in an Afghan rebel camp, or the plight of a town awash in toxic wastes, or the impact of urbanization on a Brazilian tribe. This is the fundamental direct research mode used by humans everywhere. Everyone is a participant observer, at least in his or her own culture. When we check out a new health club, or explore a new shopping mall, or have someone over for dinner to see how we'd get along, we are employing rudimentary aspects of this mode. Participant observation is also the basic procedure through which most people "learn the ropes" in new situations as they progress through their lives. But to be sound, and to avoid blunders and blinders, participant observation must pay heed to established guidelines for each of the research elements. This mode has sometimes been maligned as being "soft," but it has produced an impressive body of works in every field. To gain a better grasp of this mode, we can contrast it with survey research.

Survey research is usually rather large-scale and therefore requires a team of researchers, whereas participant observation studies are usually quite intensive mappings of particular ongoing scenes and may thus require only a single researcher. Compare, for example, a national poll of current public opinion on Mideast questions with an in-depth investigation of how some American-based corporation deals with Mideast clients. Survey research does not require of the researcher any sustained social interaction with persons studied, whereas participant observation always requires development of personal relationships with many or all of the subjects. Survey research rarely employs more than one method of data collection, but multiple methods are always required in participant observation studies. Survey research requires complete standardization of every aspect of the data collection process, whereas participant observation requires a readiness to alter and adapt any aspect of the research at every point. And whereas survey research is statistical and quantitative, participant observation is heavily qualitative and quasistatistical in nature.

What we must appreciate is that these sharp contrasts in characteristic style do not reflect mere differences in the personal tastes and styles of researchers but instead stem from very different logics of inquiry.

SYSTEM OF INTERRELATED PARTS

Participant observation depends upon conceptualizing what's being studied as *a system of interrelated parts* rather than as a population of objects. Although it is entirely legitimate and often useful to think of, say, an organism as being a collection of cells that vary somewhat in various characteristics (as survey research would have it), it is equally legitimate and useful to think of that same organism as being an interdependent system of functional organs. The idea of *systems* has proved quite useful in any number of fields of learning, from engineering through biology to linguistics. Participant observation, however, is a way of studying *social systems* of all kinds—social organizations, social activities, social settings, social situations, cultures, and the like. For example, a city need not be thought of only as a population of persons but may be viewed alternatively as some sort of dynamic community system, made up of some sorts of interrelated parts (leaders, influentials, and followers) working together to create and maintain a distinctive community. A congregation might not be viewed just as a population of members, but alternatively as a dynamic, functioning system that serves various purposes and has complex influences upon the lives of the participants.

Such a fundamental conceptualization leads to somewhat distinctive basic aims of inquiry, namely, to describe the workings of a social system. Description here must go beyond the sort of statistical description encountered in survey research to what might be called *analytic description.* That is, before we can describe the workings of a system, we must first properly analyze the system to identify what it is that serves as its functional parts before we can begin to empirically describe their interrelations. Social theories about various kinds of social systems can provide useful clues here, but more helpful is the fact that social systems (unlike mechanical or biological systems) can directly report many aspects of their own structure. That is, the workings of all social systems centrally depend upon the existence of shared understandings, meanings, expectations, and rules. By taking the trouble to learn these cultural elements, the researcher can grasp the basis and rationale for the division of labor; the local culture of the social system usually names the different parts played in its workings. The researcher may then need only to conceptually refine this identification of parts provided him or her by the local culture, so that he or she may go on to empirically and objectively describe structural and functional interrelations among those parts. To sum up, the basic aims of inquiry in participant observation research are to develop an analytic description of system properties of a particular social system.

From such analytic descriptions, explanations of how and why certain events occur can often be developed. For example, we may discover the actual basis (as opposed to the PR) upon which individuals are promoted or deadended in various types of organizations. Through participant observation we have come to understand many of the regularities that hold true for any kind of social organization. We have also come to know something about differences in the workings of different types of organizations, such as large versus small or autocratic versus democratic.

The ordinary person utilizes this research mode in a far more intuitive and haphazard fashion, noting perhaps only that it's more fun at one amusement park than another, or that raises and promotions come more easily at one company than another. The practitioner uses this mode to ferret out difficulties that can then be treated with his or her technology to increase some desired factor such as efficiency, higher cash flows, or better health. This mode can be employed with any organization of interworking parts, under any set of circumstances the researcher can gain access to, from couples to congresses to worldwide configurations.

By using this mode we can see the whole of some system as a configuration of interacting parts. These parts usually differ markedly from one another in both form and function. And the relationships among these parts may take any of a thousand and one different forms. Such things are what the participant observer goes forth to find out.

EFFECT ON BASIC ELEMENTS OF RESEARCH

How does this general research logic affect the shape taken by each (and all) of the eight basic elements of research, to produce such a sharply distinctive style or flavor?

The element of *questions* is heavily influenced and bounded by the underlying conceptualization and aims of participant observation, so that the research question must assume the general form of "How does this thing work as a social system?" This general question becomes a sizable set of specific questions on how the system hangs together (or, perhaps, why it doesn't) guided by the emphasis of the particular inquiry. In sharp contrast with the survey and experimental modes, these original questions undergo frequent change as the research progresses and new data come to light. "How does this system work?" may in the end become "How does management get its orders carried out?" or "How does this deviant subculture handle contrary and unfavorable inputs from the larger society?" But all along this process, the questions must remain objective and empirically answerable.

The requisite *resources* are shaped by the requirements of the basic aims of inquiry, namely, that the researcher take the time to learn the local culture and to then stick around long enough to empirically describe the interrelations among the parts of the system. Learning a culture may be most effectively achieved by a single mind, and it may be inefficient to tie up a large number of researchers for a project of such small scale and relatively long duration. Moreover, in order to stick around long enough, the researcher must create enduring personal relationships with those being studied; these difficulties multiply geometrically with the number of researchers. Thus, participant observation tends to be long-term solo research and is fairly demanding of the human resources of the solo researcher. One must be flexible enough to devote a stretch of one's life, to adapt to a new culture, and to develop and maintain a whole new set of personal relationships, yet be independent-minded enough to maintain some scientific objectivity and avoid "going native." Although material resources are not so demanding in this mode, and large numbers of personnel are not required, the human resources of interpersonal skills are at a premium because access to scenes usually considered private must be continually negotiated. Access also involves environmental resources, including permissions from some authorities.

Sampling becomes rather complex in participant observation research. Until the researcher has attained a useful analytic identification of the parts of the system, his or her selection of information sources is geared toward generating ideas and insights (theoretical sampling). Only later does one's sampling become statistically rigorous, as one seeks an adequate, unbiased, and representative set of data describing the interrelations among all the system parts. As an illustration, one might first investigate the layout and routines of a singles bar, and then go on to sample the interactions among the different types of customers, the staff, and the management, over a period of time. One might thus discover regulars who are more or less insiders and casual customers who are more or less prey.

These phases of sampling therefore dictate similar phases in *data collection;* the researcher's plans for evoking and selecting data must be flexible and somewhat open-ended as long as one is still seeking to get a conceptual grasp of the system, but become rather more structured when one turns to the task of empirically describing interrelations among system parts. Even then, however, the participant observer's data collection plans rarely approach the explicit standardization characteristic of survey research, because of the need to employ multiple methods for collecting data. Direct observation obviously is central to participant observation research, but this method cannot be relied upon exclusively. Social system events often take place simultaneously in different locations; the system has been functioning long before the researcher ever took up its study; and many of the most important features of the system (meanings, motivations, intentions, expectations, perceptions, interpretations) can be only imperfectly observed. For these reasons the researcher must often resort to various kinds of interviewing and to analysis of documents (for example, minutes of meetings, diaries, rulebooks) to fill in the gaps in the observational record and to supplement imperfect observations. This necessary lack of high standardization in the evoking and selecting of data in turn precludes the highly standardized plans for encoding and recording of data that are typical of survey research. Precoded instruments for data collection can play little part; instead, most data are first recorded in the form of narrative field notes and only later systematically encoded and rerecorded.

The researcher must be particularly alert to blunders and blinders in both sampling and data gathering when employing this mode. The unusual and dramatic situation can be mistaken for the typical; the public relations front can be mistaken for the real story; important echelons of the organization can be entirely missed; and so on. Also, the blunders and blinders of one's informants must often be overcome if objectivity is to be achieved. However, if these barriers can be overcome, the researcher may emerge with a portrayal of a live system unrivaled by any other research mode.

Because data collection in participant observation research cannot be highly standardized, *measurement* cannot often depend on exacting, standardized patterns of indicators in classifying cases. Reliance on more flexible patterns of indicators not only makes it difficult to attain interval and ratio-scale measurements, but also opens the door to questions about the consistency, meaningfulness, and objectivity with which classification decisions were made. Bias is a serious possibility, if only because of the culture shock the researcher will have experienced and because of the personal relationships he or she will have developed with those being studied. Reliability of measurement procedures is also more difficult to demonstrate when flexible patterns of indicators are relied upon and when only one researcher has a hand in the classification decisions.

In this mode particularly, the researcher must often focus on how the participants in the system classify and measure one another. Although such gradings are usually only at the ordinal or even nominal level, they are often of crucial importance in understanding how the system works.

Given the rather qualitative character of measurement, truly statistical analysis of data is severely limited in participant observation research. Instead, quasi-statistical patterns are sought extensively, through analysis procedures that more nearly resemble Bayesian than classical statistical analysis. Also, the system focus of participant observation research attaches considerable interest in the search for purely qualitative patterns. Apart from its generally qualitative character, data analysis in participant observation is intertwined to an unusual degree with the elements of questions, sampling, and data collection. Analysis of data is not deferred until all the data are in hand. Ideally, all the data are reanalyzed every day, in light of the newest additions, to see which research questions may have been resolved, how other questions should be revised, and whether new questions arise. This new picture then suggests what further data should be collected, from which types of source, in order to pursue the current set of questions. Here, particularly, we can see the intertwining of all our research elements.

The element of evaluation is quite as prominent in participant observation as it is in any other research, but the shape of the foregoing elements dictates distinctive concerns. Because of the comparative lack of standardization, conventional tools for assessing control of sampling error, measurement error, and analysis error are almost impossible to apply in evaluating participant observation research. In their stead, the participant observer tends to rely on an almost obsessive process of cross-checking his or her data. On a particular research question, do each of the methods of data collection yield results that agree closely with one another? Do the data from one source agree closely with those from all other relevant sources? Have any potential sources been overlooked that might provide yet another cross-check? The specters of bias and unreliability drive the participant observer to almost incredible lengths in these efforts to demonstrate the soundness and accuracy of the results. In determining the meanings and implications of his or her results, the participant observer usually compares findings with data from other systems and with social science theories about systems generally. Thus, the study is fit into the wider scene in the hope that understanding is enhanced.

The element of communication also displays distinctive aspects in participant observation research. First of all, the necessity for the researcher to learn the local culture of the social system under study shows the temendous importance of evoking and receiving communications from the inhabitants and any other useful informants. Through such backgrounding inputs, the prevailing mental conceptions of those being studied exert powerful influence on how the researcher analyzes that system. Second, the personal relationships one necesarily develops with those being studied are often felt as a serious constraint on one's eventual reports; the participant observer typically feels that whatever one says about that social system might in some way or other hurt all or some of those subjects one has become close to. The reports therefore may omit or de-emphasize certain facts, and every effort will be made to disguise the identity of persons studied—and perhaps even the system as a whole. Third, the very aim of participant observation research (to analytically describe the detailed structure and functioning of a social system), together with the qualitative and unstandardized nature of its results and the obsessive cross-checking typical of the evaluation element, dictates a comparatively discursive, densely documented, and therefore lengthy report. Qualitative data and analyses cannot so easily be compacted into summary statistics, tables, and charts. Because these reports are long and complex, the information they contain may become less accessible to interested consumers. On the other hand, their rich qualitative detail very often makes such reports excellent reading.

By fully grasping the basic guidelines for each of the elements and by paying close attention to them throughout the research process, participant observers can and do achieve professional research results that have contributed greatly to the wheel of collective human intelligence. These results then become backgrounding for further research in whichever mode.

CHAPTER

14

EXPERIMENTS

Experimentation—manipulating something to see what then happens—is quite as fundamental to intelligence as are the other modes of inquiry we have discussed. Children, monkeys, and raccoons, for example, are inveterate experimenters. And many features of the world—faucets, light switches, TV knobs—practically invite manipulation, which often leads to dramatically striking effects. The impulse to generalize findings is just as evident in experimentation as in other modes of inquiry. When the child or the monkey has satisfied himself that turning this faucet in this direction leads to water coming out, he generalizes that expectation to all faucets.

The logic of experimentation, then, rests on a hybrid conceptualization of the subject matter being studied, namely, a population of systems view. As in survey research, the interest in generalizing findings requires thinking of what is being studied as an identifiable population of basically similar entities, but here each of these entities is viewed not as a stable object but as a dynamic system in the same sense as in participant observation. For example, rather than view individuals or small groups as fairly stable objects varying in certain characteristics, one might view an individual as a personality system or think of a jury or a family as a social system. When the subject matter can be construed as such a population of systems, the distinctive aims of experimental inquiry are to do something to some of these systems and find out how systems of this kind respond to it in comparison with systems not so treated.

Experimentation involves some kind of active intervention in events. Its utterly basic form goes, "if we do X, how will this affect Y?" If a housewife adds garlic powder to her usual chili recipe, will her family like it more? Less? No difference? If people take vitamin E, will this significantly reduce the incidence of heart troubles? From time immemorial, human beings have sought laws where they can depend on the fact that if they do X they will produce effect Y. The experimental mode involves the notions of time, cause, and effect—what effect will the action of certain factors have upon the subsequent state of other factors? The experimental researcher seeks to test the influence of some factors or variables upon others by rigorously controlling the impingement of the causal variables upon the effect variables, and by eliminating as much as possible any extraneous influences.

The classic form of the professional experiment is utterly simple. We have two supposedly similar groups; one group we treat in some way, the other we don't. Then we look for some subsequent significant difference between the two groups, supposedly resulting from the treatment. This mode lends itself beautifully and directly to the standard scientific empirical question—the classic causal hypothesis. More elaborate experimental designs simply add more layers to this classic design; thus, the effects of one or more treatments on different types of groups can be studied and the influence of additional variables can be looked at. But simple or complex, all design forms within the experimental mode seek to deal with the bogey of contamination, where the results are masked, washed out, distorted, or produced by influences other than the treatment.

PRETESTING AND POSTTESTING

The central difficulty in experimental inquiry is being able to tell whether the behavior of the system after the manipulation is truly a response to that manipulation. The experimenter is in very much the same intellectual situation as the angry child who wishes his father were dead, and shortly thereafter the father does die; was the death in response to the wish? The experimenter is haunted by the possibility that the system would have behaved the way it did even if the manipulation had never taken place. He needs, then, some solidly grounded model of how the system would have looked without the prior manipulation. In some fields (for example, parts of physics), our practical and theoretical knowledge of certain systems is so well established that we know with great confidence what the system would have looked like without the manipulation, but such would almost never be so in social research. Instead, we must rely on more empirical estimates of what the system would have looked like without the manipulation.

One type of empirical estimate is the pretest. That is, take a good look at the system before the manipulation and assume that that is pretty much how the system would have looked later had it not been manipulated. Such assumptions of stability, inertia, or continuity can be quite defensible in certain subject matters. For example, if this rock has looked this way for hundreds of years now, it almost certainly would have looked that way for another hour if we hadn't poured this acid on it. But these same assumptions are much less defensible in the case of poorly understood and highly dynamic personality or social systems. Just because this five-year-old child has never yet been able to read, it would be unwise to suppose that he would still be unable to read at age six if we had not put him through this experimental school curriculum. Given the other factors in his modern environment and the continuing rapid development of his brain, he might very well have acquired some reading ability even without our manipulation.

A second empirical means of estimating what the system would have looked like is to take a good look, later on, at an identical system that did not receive the manipulation. The difficulty, of course, is that no two persons (families or juries) are identical; even if they were true clones, they will surely have differing histories of experience with the environment that will affect their dynamic functioning. Any two systems, no matter how similar, could reasonably be expected to differ in some ways at a later date even if neither received the experimental manipulation.

Much scientific experimentation in social research relies on combining these two imperfect estimators so that the strengths of one largely offset the weaknesses of the other. That is, the manipulated and the unmanipulated systems are both pretested and posttested. Then the pretest-to-posttest change observed for the unmanipulated system serves as a more realistic baseline model for how the manipulated system might have changed had it not received the manipulation. An observed difference between their respective change scores is a fairly strong argument that the manipulation produced a genuine response.

But there still remains the possibility that the two systems, no matter how similar they were shown to be at the time of pretesting, might yet have diverged in their development regardless of the manipulation, because the pretesting can only establish similarity in a limited number of observable characteristics. Here, sampling theory comes to the rescue, by showing how much safety there is in large numbers. If a sufficiently large group of systems is chosen to receive the manipulation and a comparably large group of systems is chosen to remain unmanipulated, and if these two groups are formed through strict probability sampling procedures (random assignment), then one can be practically certain that the two groups will prove equivalent in both observed and unobserved characteristics. Thus we might randomly divide a large class into two groups, give a special training regimen to one but not the other, and test for subsequent differences in reading skills between the two groups. This is the classic experimental model at work.

To assure the *continuing* equivalence of the two groups, however, requires that their ongoing experiences with the environment be kept as similar as possible except for receiving or not receiving the manipulation. For this reason, most experiments are conducted within a laboratory setting, where what happens to the two groups can be controlled and monitored by the experimenter. Because individuals and small groups have outside involvements and obligations, it is rarely possible to confine them to the laboratory setting for any great length of time, however. And some systems (armies, hospitals, police departments) are too large or too intricately involved with an external environment for us to be able to bring them within a laboratory setting.

To overcome these limitations of the laboratory, social researchers have turned increasingly to field experiments conducted in natural settings. For instance, randomly selected Army platoons might be treated with teaching machine instruction, and their performance over a subsequent one-year period compared with that of the randomly selected platoons that did not receive this additional training. Such field experiments may escape the artificiality of the laboratory setting, but they also escape the stringent controls possible in the lab. In field settings, the experimenter cannot do much to control the experiences of the two groups but can only monitor these experiences. The specter of contamination of results by other factors (such as the mere fact of having been singled out for experimental treatment) must continually be wrestled with by the field experimenter. Yet, he or she has the advantage that lengthier studies can be undertaken, in conditions that much more closely approximate those of the real world.

In all of these procedures one can see the striving to attain as closely as possible the classical experimental form. These procedures are not perfect but they have proven quite workable in all of the social sciences. The most dangerous departure from the classic form (and the procedure most used by untrained laymen) is to deal with only one group or one case, carry out some manipulation, and then generalize from the observed results. This procedure is the riskiest of all because it provides no safeguards against contamination of the findings by other influences.

CHARACTERISTICS OF EXPERIMENTATION

The general logic of experimentation imparts a rather distinctive style, or flavor, to the research enterprise. The hybrid conceptualization on which experimentation rests combines some stylistic flavor of survey research with some of that of participant observation, yet closely resembles neither. Like survey research, experimentation is thoroughly quantitative in its concern with statistical description and explanation, sampling theory, and obsessive standarization of all procedures. Like participant observation, however, experimentation devotes its primary attention to studying dynamic system properties and looks to an understanding of system functioning to account for system response to manipulations. Yet, experimentation prefers an outsider's view of systems (unlike participant observation), takes a different slice across both statistics and sampling theory than does survey research, and exceeds even survey research in its obsession with standardization by trying to lend strict uniformity not only to data collection and measurement but also the environment and experiences of those being studied.

All this can be better appreciated through a closer look at the shape assumed by the several elements of research. Most critical, perhaps, is the form assumed by the element of questions. Although cause-effect questions can be and are addressed in other modes of social research, experimentation is strictly limited to cause-effect questions, of two general forms. The less focused of these is the form:

"What are the effects on Q-type systems of doing X to them?" The more directively focused is the form: "Does doing X to Q-type systems lead to system response Y?" Although these question forms appear applicable to a rather broad range of subject matters, they are nevertheless more limited than some other cause-effect questions in that the only type of causal factor these permit is doing something to a system—that is to say, administering a treatment or manipulation. The scope of experimentation is thus limited to studying the effects of what can be feasibly manipulated; practical, technological, legal, ethical, and even logical constraints on what can be manipulated set real bounds on which causal factors can be studied experimentally. Ingenious researchers have often stretched these bounds, but we cannot, for example, treat a random group of families with disruptive stress to see how many will break up at what speed.

The element of resources is affected less clearly, except to note that resources will be needed to carry out the manipulation as well as to study its consequences. The population of systems idea implies that an experiment will need a larger number of cases than participant observation, though usually fewer than survey research. Because of the difficulties of controlling and monitoring the environment and experiences of systems, few experiments involve even moderately long periods of time. Few cases and short times translate into small research teams and relatively low personnel costs, but the desirability of environmental control leads to investments in laboratory facilities and equipment. The controlling (not to say manipulative) role of the experimenter leads to greater social distance between researcher and subjects.

In recent years, some very long-term studies have been launched, often combining laboratory and field experimentation. Many of these are in the health field, but often have sociological aspects as well. These studies usually involve large resources and huge fundings and may require virtually a career commitment on the part of the personnel. But such huge undertakings are still very much the exception for the experimental mode.

The population focus of experimentation lends considerable importance to the element of sampling; yet in practice careful sampling of cases often has taken a backseat to the assignment of sampled subjects to treatments. It is a familiar truism that experimental psychology is the science of college sophomores, so that its results have often proved difficult to generalize accurately to other subjects, settings, and historical times. This is a beautiful example of the weakness of expediency sampling. Often the experimental sample is not broad enough to fit the shape of the population we wish to draw conclusions about. Only recently have many experimenters begun to take this difficulty seriously and engage in more rigorous sampling procedures.

With respect to the element of data collection, it should be emphasized that experimentation is a quite general logic of inquiry that does not strongly favor any particular method of data collection. In an experiment the data may be collected by means of direct observation, interviewing, questionnaires and tests, existing documents, or any combination of these methods. The statistical aims of experimentation dictate that data collection be highly standardized; thus the selection, encoding, and recording of data closely resemble those in survey research. It is the aspect of evoking data that is most distinctive in experimentation; to speak of administering a manipulation to see how a system responds makes clear that data collection in experiments involves a potent evoking (almost provoking) of data flow.

Measurement in experimentation is equally rigorous and exacting, as in survey research, with respect to measuring the effects (or dependent variables) of the manipulation. However, because the experimenter usually delivers the manipulation (independent variable), he has not tended to feel it necessary to actually measure the independent variable. In studying the effects of fear arousal on the leadership structure of groups, for example, the experimenter might manipulate fear arousal by blowing dark smoke under the laboratory door while ringing an alarm bell. Too often, the experimenter would take it for granted that this manipulation aroused fear, when in fact only some or even no subjects became fearful. Only recently have many experimenters come to see that it is just as necessary to measure what happens to a system as it is to measure what the system then does. That is, until recently, experimenters tended to assume that their manipulations were what they were intended to be and that the effects of these manipulations were uniform across subjects.

Analysis of experimental data is thoroughly statistical but employs different statistical methods from those most commonly used in survey research. Unlike the correlational methods of survey analysis, experimental statistics (such as analysis of variance techniques) are designed to statistically explain measured differences within the sample of cases in terms of the effects of membership in the manipulated versus unmanipulated groups.

The statistical aims of experimentation impart to the element of evaluation a focus on the control and assessment of measurement error, sampling error, and analysis errors. An extremely deep concern for standardization in all steps and procedures of the research process is a necessary concomitant, and it has already been noted that this extends beyond standardizing the data to standardizing the environment and experiences of the subjects. But the most distinctive focus of evaluation in experimentation centers on the logical and practical difficulties of determining whether system behavior is a response to the manipulation—that is, in being able to determine what the system would have looked like if it had not received the manipulation.

Communication of the results of an experiment is highly conventionalized (therefore relatively easy) and comparatively brief (because the research question is often a more or less yes-no form: Does doing X to such systems lead to Y?). For these reasons, publication and dissemination of results is relatively inexpensive and straightforward. Because of the prestige of experimentation, wider audiences frequently grant more automatic credence to experimental results than is actually warranted. For instance, a rigorous experiment involving college sophomores does not generalize very well to any larger population, except perhaps other sophomores at that school. No professional survey researcher or participant observer would make such an error.

The very stringency of experimental methods that often makes them so difficult to adapt to live situations is also their strength. A classic experiment has a clean elegance for explaining things and for verifying notions that can rise far above our ordinary "fish and fumble" thinking about the world. Clever researchers are learning more and more how to apply this mode—long the darling of the physical sciences—to the sphere of social research.

Again, no mode is better than the rest; rather, each will do a particular kind of job especially well in our quest to find out.

Each of the four major modes of social research can be harnessed to do the work of expanding our collective knowledge. But, in themselves, they are only passive blueprints for inquiry. They must be brought to life by our hybrid scholar/adventurer, plying his craft.

PART IV

CREATIVE INQUIRY

Research is not a mechanical process, suitable for turning over to some programmed computer. It is instead a skilled and creative process, rooted in the very nature of intelligence. Research vitally involves discipline and rules, but we have already seen that discipline is fundamental to the very nature of intelligence and that the rules of inquiry are like the rules of cooking or carpentry rather than the rules of a monastery.

In the concluding Chapter 15, we examine more closely the highly personal and creative nature of social research, rejecting an industrial conception of research in favor of a view of research as a craft endeavor, augmenting and harnessing human creativity.

CHAPTER
15
THE CRAFT OF FINDING OUT

Craftsmanship, in any field, requires trained discipline with the tools of the trade, on the one hand, and artistic creativity on the other. And so it is with social research.

Finding out is a matter of producing knowledge. Is knowledge the sort of thing that can be cranked out through application of mechanical procedures, or is it instead something that must be discovered by breakthrough insights of great thinkers? Actually, it is neither and both. Finding out—in daily life and in social research—requires a mix of technical discipline with creative or artistic judgment. Too much artistry produces a wildness and unreliability, and too much discipline produces a dull and plodding robotism. Ungrounded speculation, and unimaginative, disciplined conservatism have alike produced little advance in our wheel of collective human intelligence and have, in fact, often led humankind astray.

The mass media often speak of the knowledge industry, the complex of giant research and development firms, universities, and federal laboratories that together underlie the knowledge explosion and fuel the modern Information Society. Is knowledge the sort of thing that can be mass-produced on an assembly-line basis? Or is knowledge instead the product of a true craftsman, a single individual who maintains the mental image of a completed product from start to finish and who knows everything that goes into it even if some of the work is performed by others? There is some truth to both views. Much important knowledge today is produced routinely through the ongoing, standardized operations of large-scale shops within the knowledge industry. Yet, much of the most innovative knowledge remains the product of individuals. If we look closely at the successes, in either case, we will see real craftsmanship at work.

> Craftmanship follows a plan devised by the worker. This plan, whether it is the pattern for carving a rocking chair or the design for examining a social problem, is of course shaped by the worker's prior experience. A researcher may use a theory that has been used before, in the same manner as the carpenter decides to make another chair like the one in his parlor. But the plans of both are also highly individualistic, and subject to modification as the work progresses. The result, therefore, reveals the personality and interests of the worker. The scientific canon of objectivity does not mean that research has to be uniform and colorless. The difference between ordinarily and finely crafted studies is comparable to the distinction between mass-produced and one-of-a-kind items. In spite of the freedom to create which craftsmanship affords, there is, inevitably, some mechanical drudgery in some phases of the work. However, says [C. Wright] Mills, the craftsman is "carried over these junctures by keen anticipation" of what the finished product will look like, and by pride at its completion.*

In this concluding chapter, we examine social research as a skilled craft in just this sense, combining the discipline imposed by the rules of research with the personal and creative art of finding out.

There is much popular mystery surrounding science and research. Great scientists are sometimes regarded with awe and wariness as a breed apart, almost as if they existed on some other plane of reality from you and me. But so are great artists in every field, including those who are true artists in the kitchen. A great cook "may seem like a magician, adding a 'pinch of this' and a 'dash of that.' She may claim that intuition tells her when the oven is hot enough or when the baked apples are soft enough."† Such amazing abilities, of cook or scientist, do not reflect any particular genetic or supernatural giftedness but rather reflect the imagination, inspiration, and implicit knowledge acquired through patient mastery of the craft. The abilities of a master craftsman dazzle us only because we are amateurs; fellow

---

* Williamson, Karp, Dalphin, and Gray, *The Research Craft*, p. 30.

† Ibid., p. 37.

craftsmen may be impressed and even envious, but they will not usually be dazzled or amazed.

Much of the social research one encounters is quite ordinarily crafted—more or less soundly done, but routine and humdrum, each very much like a hundred other studies. This is essentially "cookbook research," in which journeyman researchers replicate kitchen-tested recipes (developed by others), using off-the-shelf or canned materials (measures, statistical routines, and sampling frames). Little creative judgment or artistry is evident in such by-the-book research. It is like the quite ordinary cooking done by someone who recently acquired a charcoal grill, which came with a booklet of instructions and recipes. Following this booklet, practically anyone can manage to turn out a limited range of more or less edible dishes. Such productions are, of course, still far superior to the work of the untrained amateur, who can barely cook at all and who may well produce dangerous fare. A true cook, however, will quickly see some novel and promising possibilities in this tool far beyond the sorts envisioned in the booklet, adapting quite different dishes to the requirements of this mode of cooking. Still, it would take a real artist to make a souffle on a charcoal grill.

THE CREATIVE RESEARCH PROCESS

Granted that there is an art of finding out, how does one ever manage to progress from cookbook researcher to skilled craftsman? How does one acquire the intricately structured implicit knowledge that inspires the sound imaginativeness of the master?

A good understanding of a social science discipline is first, because such a disciplinary framework provides the tools for the creative research process. Just as one must learn the rules, the board, and the pieces before one can strive to be a good chess player, so a grasp of one's discipline is a necessary but not sufficient condition for creative work. One does not want to be simultaneously fumbling with one's tools while trying to carry out the investigative enterprise.

In acquiring any craft, there is the matter of instruction and practice—hopefully with different mentors and under different circumstances, adding both depth and breadth to one's apprenticeship. This will acquaint the fledgling with the backgroundings necessary for forging ahead or resolving particular practical cases, and will prevent him or her from naively struggling to reinvent arithmetic. Also, it will provide a repertoire of different angles or conceptual models for viewing slices of reality.

The matter of practice shades into the factor of experience. There is no proven substitute for experience; folk wisdom is correct in holding that experience is the best teacher and that beyond a certain point one learns by doing. One becomes smoother, more efficient, and experiences an ever-widening range of circumstances that require the creative adaptation of operating routines. In-depth familiarity with any area is a key factor in creativity and a principal by-product of experience. Experience depends on dedication and persistence. Persistence in a subject area, although it sometimes borders on obsession or monomania, allows for the slow accumulation of insights and data and for a long enough incubation period. Although many people may be quite interested in a subject area, most burn out, give up, and move on before acquiring sufficient experience to rise to the level of craftsman.

Closely allied with experience is experimenting. By sticking with it long enough, one encounters many different situations and circumstances that require adaptive response—that is, trying something a little different. The skilled craftsman will have tried out many little wrinkles over the years, will have learned that many of these innovations don't work (and why they don't), and will have through experience developed enough confidence to experiment again under practically any circumstances.

Finally, there is the factor of continual and extensive communication, both with self and with others. Communication with oneself is vital; one who aspires to master a craft must constantly be reflecting on what one might do, on why something one tried turned out the way it did, and on how and why some other craftsman did what he did. Reflection is critical to mastery. Communication with other craftsmen is also vital. Dedicated reading, for example, is fundamental. Although one of the things about a master cook that impresses the amateur is that the master is rarely observed following any recipe, you may count on the fact that the master cook has accumulated and digested a vast library of recipes and books on cooking that serves both to inform and to inspire his or her own creative efforts. More direct communication between fellow craftsmen is also important; as they examine one another's products, chat together, and observe one another working, each is continually searching for tips on new techniques and new product ideas. Talking shop among fellow craftsmen is, no doubt, as old as the human race and has contributed much to its forward process.

Even though many master researchers, like many master cooks, have chosen to specialize in one particular style or mode, their communication practices are seldom tightly confined. A dedicated survey researcher will keep up with those aspects of experimental work that might someday prove useful to his own work, just as a master of French cooking will maintain an interest in certain facets of Portuguese cuisine.

Researchers may sometimes appear to be lonely persons, going their own way, but a closer inspection of their habits reveals that they are in extensive communication within the areas of their interests. Through such extensive and intensive communications, the craftsman excels over others in his or her backgrounding; his knowledge is "state of the art" right up with the forward edge of the wheel of collective human intelligence.

DEPTH AND BREADTH OF KNOWLEDGE

The sound imaginativeness that is the creative element in the art of finding out seems, then, to depend on both depth and breadth of knowledge. Depth of knowledge contributes particularly to the soundness of the work by helping to ensure that it is well grounded and not naive through sheer ignorance of what has already been done and established by others. Such in-depth knowledge also tends to increase the cost-efficiency of resource utilization.

Breadth of knowledge contributes particularly to the imaginativeness of any endeavor. Broadening the scope of one's knowledge about a particular subject seems to involve a grab bag of things, such as savvy in two or more fields, where each can provide some fresh perspectives on the other. Included also would be extensive reading in many different areas, travel, friends and acquaintances in different careers and from different walks of life, hobbies that input a range of data and ideas from fields beyond the subject under inquiry. All these seem to enable the inquirer to make connections among disparate items and to produce more flexibility and agility of viewpoint, approach, and design.

Breakthroughs are the gemstones of inquiry—those major shifts in knowledge, whether in science or in someone's personal life career. But how do we bring them about? This question probably can never be answered fully, because such momentous results from an inquiry seem to involve the highest abilities attained by human beings, a realm not well understood at all.

However, a number of things can be safely said about breakthroughs on the basis of examining some of those who have made them. First, the person has usually really done his or her homework, often many years of it. As we look at the real research craftsmen, we see long-term questing attributes manifested. The hunches, intuitions, and inductive leaps that eventually prove to be valid advances in our knowledge seem to be fed by a thorough, continuing grounding in the area coupled with a latent learning incubation period of mulling over the subject.

Second, breakthroughs often display a shocking quality. They almost inevitably involve some fundamental change in our conceptions of the environment. So they often require "thinking the unthinkable" and thus demand some independence of spirit on the part of the inquirer, because these new conceptions will fly in the face of the common sense prevailing in that historical neck of the woods. (After all, any fool can look out his window and see that the earth is flat and that the sun and stars revolve around us.) Such an innovative inquirer is likely to regarded as "off-center" during the stages of his or her investigation and the results are likely to be revolutionary by definition. It is interesting to realize that a great many of our cornerstone notions about the world were considered crackpot when they first appeared.

A study of history demonstrates that even scientists and scholars have often been stuck in a conservative, even resistive track, and in such cases the research community can act as a brake as much as a support for the forward progress of our wheel. No doubt, many of the conceptions we hold as truths today will be utterly overturned or surprisingly refined by tomorrow's researchers.

Above and beyond the tools of the trade, there is, then, a *spirit of inquiry*. The rules of research are only the road maps; they do not describe or predetermine the journey of the wayfarer.

SUGGESTED READINGS

The argument of our book is that the rules and guidelines of social research harness the powers of ordinary human intelligence and are made necessary by the universal flaws in human intelligence. The more you know about these powers and these flaws, the more fully you will be able to grasp and profit from this book. Therefore, the most important outside reading you can undertake is reading about the workings of the human mind. The most readable, comprehensive, and up-to-date account is Morton Hunt's *The Universe Within: A New Science Explores the Human Mind* (New York: Simon and Schuster, 1982).

CHAPTER 1: TRUTHS AND CONSEQUENCES

The excitement and the fun of research, together with its rule-guided nature, led Garvin McCain and Erwin M. Segal to write about *The Game of Science* (Belmont, California: Brooks/Cole, 1969), a light-hearted and humorously illustrated analysis of the critical features distinguishing science from other human enterprises.

CHAPTER 2: THE NATURE OF RESEARCH

What we have called the wheel of collective human intelligence is more fully characterized and explained in Gordon Tullock, *The Organization of Inquiry* (Durham, N.C.: Duke University Press, 1966). How researchers must coax the environment into giving up its real truths is described in Myron Glazer's account of *The Research Adventure: Promise and Problems of Field Work* (New York: Random House, 1972).

CHAPTER 3: QUESTIONS

Robin Lakoff discusses what makes for "Questionable Answers and Answerable Questions" (in Braj B. Kachru et al, *Issues in Linguistics*. Urbana: University of Illinois Press, 1973). Even more delightful reading is Stanley L. Payne's *The Art of Asking Questions* (Princeton, N.J.: Princeton University Press, 1951), a classic which is marred only by somewhat dated or old-fashioned examples. Particularly pertinent also is the little book by John P. Campbell, Richard L. Daft, and Charles L. Hulin, *What to Study: Generating and Developing Research Questions* (Beverly Hills, California: Sage Publications, 1982).

CHAPTER 4: RESOURCES

How the ways in which resources are assembled and marshaled influence the direction and success of inquiry is examined in Richard O'Toole, editor, *The Organization, Management and Tactics of Social Research* (Cambridge, Mass.: Schenkman, 1971). Effects of political and moral climates as environmental resources are examined through a series of case studies in Gideon Sjoberg, editor, *Ethics, Politics and Social Research* (Cambridge, Mass.: Schenkman, 1967).

CHAPTER 5: SAMPLING

A delightful book and cleverly illustrated answer to the mysteries of sampling is Morris J. Slonim's *Sampling in a Nutshell* (New York: Simon and Schuster, 1960).

CHAPTER 6: DATA

The information processing skills and limitations of the human mind are nicely described in Chapter 3 of Hunt's *The Universe Within* (New York: Simon and Schuster, 1982). Leonard Bickman reviews data collection through "Observational Methods" in Claire Selltiz et al, *Research Methods in Social Relations*, 3rd ed. (New York: Holt, Rinehart and Winston, 1976). Raymond L. Gorden instructs about *Interviewing:*

Strategy, Techniques and Tactics, rev. ed. (Homewood, Ill.: Dorsey Press, 1975). Many quite ingenious techniques for obtaining data are reviewed in Eugene J. Webb et al, *Unobtrusive Measures: Nonreactive Research in the Social Sciences* (Chicago: Rand McNally, 1966).

CHAPTER 7: MEASUREMENT

Most discussions of measurement tend to be rather technical in nature. You might, however, take a look at Gene F. Summers, editor, *Attitude Measurement* (Chicago: Rand McNally, 1970).

CHAPTER 8: ANALYSIS

Hunt's book provides helpful accounts (in Chapter 5) of how humans discover patterns and regularities in complex data sets and (in Chapter 4) how natural reasoning differs from technically logical reasoning. Classical statistical analysis is nicely introduced by Allan G. Johnson in *Social Statistics Without Tears* (New York: McGraw-Hill, 1977).

CHAPTER 9: EVALUATION

Some of the issues in making sense of results are discussed in Eric Donald Hirsch, Jr., *Validity in Interpretation* (New Haven: Yale University Press, 1967). An excellent guide to assessing the trustworthiness of results is Jeffrey Katzer, Kenneth H. Cook, and Wayne W. Crouch, *Evaluating Information: A Guide for Users of Social Science Research* (Reading, Mass.: Addison-Wesley, 1978).

CHAPTER 10: COMMUNICATION

There are many excellent books on how to propose and report research. But for readers of this book, communication outputs are less at issue than input processes such as reading and listening. At a fairly basic level we recommend Paul D. Leedy, *How to Read Research and Understand It* (New York: Macmillan, 1981), on the one hand, and

Ernest P. Mills, *Listening: Key to Communication* (Philadelphia: Petrocelli Books, 1974) on the other.

CHAPTER 11: SECONDARY RESEARCH AND SECONDARY ANALYSIS

We can all use a little help in looking up answers; one useful guide is Alden Todd's *Finding Facts Fast: How to Find Out What You Want and Need to Know*, 2nd ed. (Berkeley, Calif.: Ten Speed Press, 1979). To help you decide whether the answer you have looked up is sufficiently sound, we again strongly recommend Katzer, Cook, and Crouch, *Evaluating Information*. Secondary analysis is necessarily a little more technical than secondary research, but you should be able to handle Catherine Hakim's *Secondary Analysis in Social Research: A Guide to Data Sources and Methods with Examples* (London: George Allen and Unwin, 1982).

CHAPTER 12: SURVEY RESEARCH

Earl R. Babbie provides a readable and comprehensive account of *Survey Research Methods* (Belmont, Calif.: Wadsworth, 1973). A particularly interesting perspective is that of the hired interviewers, recounted with insight in Jean M. Converse and Howard Schuman, *Conversations at Random: Survey Research as Interviewers See It* (Ann Arbor: University of Michigan Institute for Survey Research, 1978).

CHAPTER 13: PARTICIPANT OBSERVATION

Naturally enough, we recommend here our own earlier book, *Issues in Participant Observation: A Text and Reader* (Reading, Mass.: Addison-Wesley, 1969). Briefer and less technical is Leonard Schatzman and Anselm L. Strauss, *Field Research: Strategies for a Natural Sociology* (Englewood Cliffs, N.J.: Prentice-Hall, 1973).

CHAPTER 14: EXPERIMENTS

A brief and readable account of the logic of experimentation and the statistical methods for analyzing data from experiments is Barry Anderson's *The Psychology Experiment*, 2nd ed. (Belmont, Calif.: Brooks/ Cole, 1971). A more human interest treatment of all stages in the process of experimental research is Kenneth Graham's *Psychological Research: Controlled Interpersonal Interaction* (Belmont, Calif.: Brooks/Cole, 1977).

CHAPTER 15: THE CRAFT OF FINDING OUT

The latest theories and findings on human creativity are reviewed in Chapter 8 of Hunt's book, mentioned earlier. D. M. Dooling provides a literary examination of craftsmanship in *A Way of Working* (Garden City, N.Y.: Doubleday Anchor, 1979). We especially recommend the classic essay of C. Wright Mills on intellectual craftsmanship in *The Sociological Imagination* (New York: Oxford Press, 1959).

Index